FEMA
Mitigation Assessment Team
Compendium Report
2017 Hurricane Season
September 2019

The purpose of this book is to summarize the observations, conclusions, and recommendations from post-disaster assessments conducted by the FEMA MAT's in response to the 2017 Hurricane Season.

It is published as a convenience to those who may wish to have a quality professionally printed copy of the manual.

Should you have suggestions or feedback on ways to improve this book please send email to Books@OcotilloPress.com

---

Edited 2021 Ocotillo Press
ISBN 978-1-954285-76-7

Ocotillo Press
Houston, TX 77017
Books@OcotilloPress.com

Disclaimer: The user of this book is responsible for following safe and lawful practices at all times. The publisher assumes no responsibility for the use of the content of this book. The publisher has made an effort to ensure that the text is complete and properly typeset, however omissions, errors, and other issues may exist that the publisher is unaware of.

2017 Hurricane Season

FEMA P-2054 / September 2019

FEMA

Any opinions, findings, conclusions, or recommendations expressed in this publication do not necessarily reflect the views of FEMA. Additionally, neither FEMA nor any of its employees makes any warranty, expressed or implied, or assumes any legal liability or responsibility for the accuracy, completeness, or usefulness of any information, product, or process included in this publication. Users of information from this publication assume all liability arising from such use.

All photographs and figures used in this report were taken by the Mitigation Assessment Team or developed for this report unless stated otherwise.

Map imagery sources (unless otherwise noted in the report):

Pre-damage aerial imagery: Google Earth Pro, http://www.google.com/enterprise/earthmaps/earthpro.html (used with license, accessed February 12, 2013, through October 25, 2013).

Pre-damage aerial imagery: Bing Maps via Esri, http://www.bing.com/maps/ (used with license, accessed February 12, 2013 through October 25, 2013).

Street maps: Esri World Street Map, http://services.arcgisonline.com/ArcGIS/rest/services/World_Street_Map/MapServer (used with license, accessed February 12, 2013 through October 25, 2013).

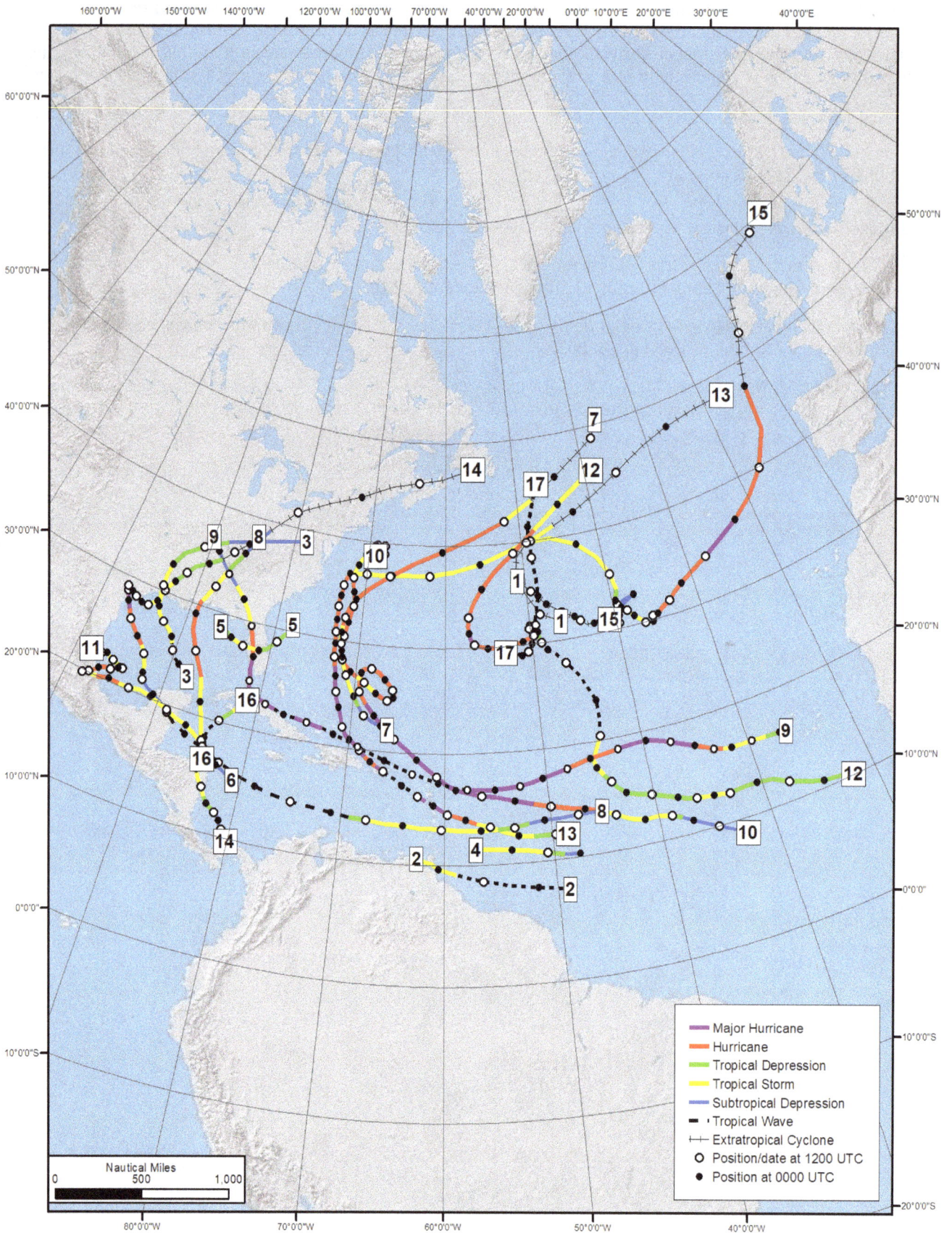

Figure ES-1: 2017 Hurricane Season Storm Tracks, April 2017–November 2017

SOURCE: NOAA NHC 2018B

MITIGATION ASSESSMENT TEAM

COMPENDIUM REPORT
2017
HURRICANE SEASON

Executive Summary

Introduction

The 2017 Atlantic hurricane season was extremely active, producing 17 named storms (Figure ES-1, Table ES-1). Six of these storms became major hurricanes (Category 3, 4, or 5), and three ranked in the National Hurricane Center's (NHC's) top five hurricanes with the greatest cumulative damage (NOAA NHC 2018a).

Table ES-1 presents the storm names correlating to the numbered labels in Figure ES-1

Table ES-1: Named Storms from the 2017 Hurricane Season

Number	Storm Name	Date	Number	Storm Name	Date
1	Arlene	April 19–21	9	Irma	August 30–September 12
2	Bret	June 19–20	10	Jose	September 5–22
3	Cindy	June 20–23	11	Katia	September 5–9
4	Don	July 17–18	12	Lee	September 14–30
5	Emily	July 30–August 1	13	Maria	September 16–30
6	Franklin	August 7–10	14	Nate	October 4–8
7	Gert	August 13–17	15	Ophelia	October 9–15
8	Harvey	August 17–September 1	16	Philippe	October 28–29
			17	Rina	November 5–9

(SOURCE: NOAA NHC 2018B)

FEMA's Mitigation Assessment Teams

For more than 30 years, the Federal Emergency Management Agency (FEMA) has been conducting studies and assessments of the performance of the built environment after disasters of national significance. In these instances, FEMA deploys Mitigation Assessment Teams (MATs) to observe building performance and provide design and construction guidance to improve disaster resistance of the built environment. This report provides a summary of the key observations and conclusions from the 2017 MAT assessments in the United States, Puerto Rico, and the U.S. Virgin Islands (USVI) following Hurricanes Harvey, Irma, and Maria.

A MAT makes observations and conducts forensic engineering analyses of building performance and related infrastructure to determine causes of damage and success, and recommends actions that federal, state, and local governments; the design and construction industry; and building code and standards organizations can take to mitigate damage from future natural hazard events. Often, FEMA will deploy a pre-Mitigation Assessment Team (pre-MAT), a small team sent in advance of the larger MAT to quickly observe and record certain perishable damage data; locate damaged areas requiring further assessment; and determine the overall impact of the hurricane, scope of buildings and areas to be visited, and building professional skillsets that would be needed for the larger, follow-on MAT.

2017 MAT Deployment

The pre-MATs and MATs deployed during the 2017 hurricane season are summarized below.

■ In response to a request for technical support from FEMA's Joint Field Office (JFO) in Austin, TX, FEMA deployed a pre-MAT to Texas in November 2017 and a MAT in December 2017 to evaluate building performance after Hurricane Harvey. The MAT was deployed to Harris County to assess flood performance issues, and to Aransas, Nueces, Refugio, and San Patricio Counties to assess wind performance issues. The MAT focused on dry floodproofing projects, residential flood- and wind-related performance, critical facilities, and other non-residential wind-related performance.

■ In response to a request for technical support from the FEMA JFO in St. Croix, USVI, FEMA deployed a MAT to affected areas in St. Thomas, St. John, and St. Croix in October 2017 and November 2017. The MAT evaluated damage from Hurricanes Irma and Maria, especially for buildings constructed or reconstructed after Hurricane Marilyn (1995), to identify both successful and unsuccessful mitigation techniques. The MAT also assessed the performance of residential, non-residential, critical facilities, and photovoltaic (PV) installations affected by the storms; and investigated the effects of wind speed-up caused by the islands' topography on building performance.

■ In coordination with the FEMA Region II office and the Puerto Rico JFO, a pre-MAT was deployed to Puerto Rico in October 2017 to evaluate building performance during Hurricanes Irma and Maria. Observations from that team led to a full MAT deployment in December 2017. Areas of focused observations included: building codes, standards, and regulations; residential and low-rise buildings; schools, critical facilities, photovoltaic (PV) arrays, siting and topography, and solar water heaters.

■ Twelve days after Hurricane Irma struck the Florida coast (September 22–25, 2017), FEMA deployed a pre-MAT to perform a preliminary field assessment of building damage in limited areas of Collier, Lee, Miami-Dade, and Monroe Counties. Following the pre-MAT, in response to a request for technical support from the JFO in Florida, FEMA deployed the full MAT in December 2017 to assess the performance of buildings in Florida. The MAT assessed flood damage related to inundation, scour, and wave forces, the performance of dry floodproofing and facility planning, and wind-related damage, with a focus on building envelope performance.

Pre-MAT and MAT members evaluated building systems to determine the effectiveness of various design and construction practices and study the effect of code adoption and enforcement on reducing flood and wind damage. To improve resiliency in future events, the lessons learned from MAT deployments and reports can be incorporated into best practices for future retrofits or incorporated into new hazard-resistant building design, among other uses.

Summary of Damage Observed by the MATs

In Texas, Hurricane Harvey caused widespread damage to buildings, power distribution systems, and water utility services in both the region impacted by its landfall and the area affected by the historic rainfall. Flood damage was extensive, impacting buildings located in the 1.0-percent-annual-chance probability (100-year event) floodplain, 0.2-percent-annual-chance probability (500-year event) floodplain, and areas well beyond the mapped floodplains. Older, slab-on-grade buildings that were not built to minimum National Flood Insurance Program (NFIP) standards sustained the most flood damage and building damage for more recently constructed buildings generally was less severe. The MAT observed failures at dry floodproofed buildings from overtopping of flood walls or barriers, structural failure of flood barriers, seepage through flood barriers, seepage through utility penetrations, and insufficient planning. Winds from Hurricane Harvey caused extensive damage to roof coverings and rooftop equipment, which resulted in rain damage to interior finishes, furnishings, and equipment. Wind-related building damage is attributable primarily to using improper materials in hurricane-prone regions, design deficiencies, poor installation, and inadequate attachment of roof coverings and roof-mounted equipment. Wind-related building envelope damage for more recently constructed residential and non-residential buildings was less severe than for older buildings.

After Hurricanes Irma and Maria, significant damage in the USVI was observed across all building types on all three of the islands. The impacts varied greatly by the building location, previous mitigation efforts, and the effectiveness of adopting recommended design standards. Numerous buildings sustained catastrophic structural damage from wind; however, many more had primary structures that performed adequately but sustained damage to roof coverings, windows, and doors that allowed wind-driven rain to infiltrate the building and damage contents. The MAT observed significant wind and water damage to schools and critical facilities in the USVI, which resulted in limitations to their emergency operations or sheltering functions during the storms. Several large, ground-mounted solar panel systems in the USVI sustained heavy damage that hindered the full return of electrical utility service to the islands.

In Puerto Rico, Hurricanes Irma and Maria caused severe damage to residential and public buildings. Flood damage was severe in some areas, while wind damage was widespread throughout the commonwealth. Hundreds of thousands of buildings were damaged and the power grid failed, causing long-lasting interruptions to essential services. Few homeowners carry flood insurance policies from the NFIP. Many homes in Puerto Rico are of informal construction (not permitted or not built to current building standards), and the residential building stock is aging. High winds caused severe damage, particularly to these informally constructed buildings and rooftop equipment. The MAT also observed settings where damage likely was caused or intensified by wind speed-up over topographic features.

In Florida, Hurricane Irma caused widespread damage to residential and commercial buildings and infrastructure. Buildings in low-lying areas were damaged from inundation, wave action, and scour. The extent of flood damage to buildings varied with the depth of floodwater, the amount of energy in the water (waves, velocity), and the nature of building design and construction (old versus new, at-grade versus elevated, manufactured housing units [MHUs] / recreational vehicle versus site-built / modular). The MAT focused primarily on one- and two-family dwellings, but also assessed some multi-family dwellings (apartments and condominiums) and MHUs. Many buildings sustained wind-induced failures of building envelope components, connections, and systems that allowed wind-driven rain to enter the interior, resulting in costly damage. While structural damage observations from Hurricane Irma winds were limited almost exclusively to pre-Florida Building Code (FBC) residential buildings, envelope damage was observed commonly on both older and newer construction. The most frequently observed damage affected roof coverings, soffits, exterior wall coverings, glazed openings, and sectional garage doors. Most observed damage to MHUs was initiated by wind acting on improperly attached appurtenances. When carports and covered porches broke away from the MHUs, they left openings at failed connections in the remaining roof or wall that allowed rain to enter the MHU envelopes.

MAT Recommendations

The recommendations presented in this report are made based on the MAT's field observations. They are directed to design professionals, contractors, building officials, facility managers, floodplain administrators, regulators, emergency managers, building owners, academia, select industries and associations, and local officials, as well as FEMA. The following three paragraphs present some of the higher priority MAT recommendations for building codes, standards, and regulations; and wind- and flood-related building performance.

Building Codes, Standards, and Regulations. Building codes, standards, and regulations should be reviewed and updated to stay consistent with the latest model building codes and referenced standards. Code enforcement staff should be trained adequately, and inspectors should ensure construction is in compliance with the applicable codes and standards for the authority having jurisdiction.

Flood-Related Building Performance. Communities and building owners should consider elevating new and Substantially Damaged / Substantially Improved buildings above the NFIP elevation requirements to protect them from flooding. Flood damage-resistant materials should be used below the design flood elevation inside dry floodproofed buildings when possible. For dry floodproofing measures, facility managers should develop an emergency operations plan that outlines how to prepare the building when severe weather is expected. Facility managers also should routinely reevaluate dry floodproofing designs and plans after deployment of their systems or training exercises and instill a culture of preparedness.

Wind-Related Building Performance. Building owners and / or facility managers should ensure roof-mounted equipment is anchored adequately and consider protecting the glazed openings on existing buildings. Windstorm inspectors and local building officials should enforce the use of approved materials in high-wind regions and ensure they are installed in accordance with the manufacturers' requirements. Contractors and inspectors also should ensure roof covering repairs and replacements are in conformance with code requirements. Design professionals, contractors, and inspectors should place more emphasis on proper soffit installation in high-wind regions to limit wind-driven rain from entering building envelopes and damaging building interiors. MHU appurtenances should be built as standalone units without structural connection to the MHU. Vulnerability assessments of roof coverings and rooftop equipment are recommended as a part of the recovery process to identify areas of weakness and needed replacement and a regular rooftop maintenance program is recommended to help identify and address weaknesses as they develop. The topographic effects of wind speed-up should be factored into building designs.

Contents

Figures

Tables

Acronyms and Abbreviations

ABFE	Advisory Base Flood Elevation
ASCE	American Society of Civil Engineers
BCEGS	Building Codes Effectiveness Grading Schedule
BFE	Base Flood Elevation
CMU	Concrete Masonry Unit
CRS	Community Rating System
DFE	Design Flood Elevation
DoD	Department of Defense
DPNR	Department of Planning and Natural Resources
EOC	Emergency Operations Center
FBC	Florida Building Code
FBCB	Florida Building Code, Building
FBCR	Florida Building Code, Residential
FBCEB	Florida Building Code, Existing Buildings
FDEM	Florida Department of Emergency Management
FEMA	Federal Emergency Management Agency
FIMA	Federal Insurance and Mitigation Administration
FIRM	Flood Insurance Rate Map
HMGP	Hazard Mitigation Grant Program
HPRP	Home Protection Roofing Program
HVHZ	High Velocity Hurricane Zone
IBC	International Building Code
IBHS	Insurance Institute for Business & Home Security
ICC	International Code Council
I-Codes	International Code Council series of codes
IRC	International Residential Code

ISO	Insurance Service Office
JFO	Joint Field Office
MAT	Mitigation Assessment Team
MEP	Mechanical, electrical, and plumbing
MHU	Manufactured housing unit
mph	Miles per hour
MWFRS	Main Wind Force Resisting System
NFIP	National Flood Insurance Program
NHC	National Hurricane Center
NOAA	National Oceanic and Atmospheric Administration
NOS	National Ocean Service
NWS	National Weather Service
OGPe	Permits Management Office (Oficina de Gerencia de Permisos)
PRBC	Puerto Rico Building Code
PREPA	Puerto Rico Electric Power Authority (Autoridad de Energía Eléctrica)
PRPB	Puerto Rico Planning Board
PV	Photovoltaic
RA	Recovery Advisory
SFHA	Special Flood Hazard Area
SMAA	State Mutual Aid Agreement
SME	Subject Matter Expert
TCPIA	Texas Catastrophe Property Insurance Association
TDI	Texas Department of Insurance
TWIA	Texas Windstorm Insurance Association
USGS	U.S. Geological Survey
USVI	United States Virgin Islands
VITEMA	Virgin Islands Territorial Emergency Management Agency

MITIGATION ASSESSMENT TEAM

COMPENDIUM REPORT
2017
HURRICANE SEASON

1 Introduction

The Federal Emergency Management Agency (FEMA), through the Building Science Branch of FEMA's Federal Insurance and Mitigation Administration (FIMA), deployed Mitigation Assessment Teams (MATs) to Texas, the U.S. Virgin Islands (USVI), Puerto Rico, and Florida in 2017 after Hurricanes Harvey, Irma, and Maria. The teams developed four MAT reports summarizing building performance observations, recommendations, and technical guidance for rebuilding:

- FEMA P-2020, *Mitigation Assessment Team Report: Hurricanes Irma and Maria in Puerto Rico (FEMA 2018a)*

- *FEMA P-2021, Mitigation Assessment Team Report: Hurricanes Irma and Maria in the U.S. Virgin Islands (FEMA 2018b)*

- *FEMA P-2022, Mitigation Assessment Team Report: Hurricane Harvey in Texas (FEMA 2019)*

- *FEMA P-2023, Mitigation Assessment Team Report: Hurricane Irma in Florida (FEMA 2018c)*

This Compendium Report summarizes the observations, conclusions, and recommendations from the four MAT reports developed for the 2017 hurricane season.

1.1   Organization of the Report

This MAT Compendium Report is divided into five chapters:

■ Chapter 1 describes the three storm events: Hurricane Harvey in Texas; Hurricane Irma in USVI, Puerto Rico, and Florida; and Hurricane Maria in USVI and Puerto Rico.

■ Chapter 2 discusses building codes, standards, and regulations in Texas, USVI, Puerto Rico, and Florida.

■ Chapter 3 describes the performance of residential, non-residential, and critical facility buildings, as well as other types of infrastructure, during the 2017 hurricanes.

■ Chapter 4 provides a summary of conclusions and recommendations and cross references to their respective MAT report(s).

■ Chapter 5 contains references.

Throughout this Compendium Report, cross-references to the four MAT reports are provided for further reading.

1.2   Purpose and Background

The purpose of this document is to summarize the observations, conclusions, and recommendations from post-disaster assessments conducted by the FEMA MATs in response to the 2017 hurricane season. More than 75 Subject Matter Experts (SMEs) were deployed to document observations, draw conclusions, and provide recommendations.

1.3   Background of the Events

This section describes each of the three major hurricanes whose damage was assessed by the MATs during the 2017 hurricane season: Hurricanes Harvey, Irma, and Maria.

1.3.1 Hurricane Harvey

1.3.1.1 Formation

Hurricane Harvey formed off the west coast of Africa on August 12, 2017 (NOAA NHC 2018c). On August 17, 2017, Harvey developed into a tropical storm that impacted the Lesser Antilles. Figure 1-1 shows Hurricane Harvey's track from August 17, 2017, through September 1, 2017.

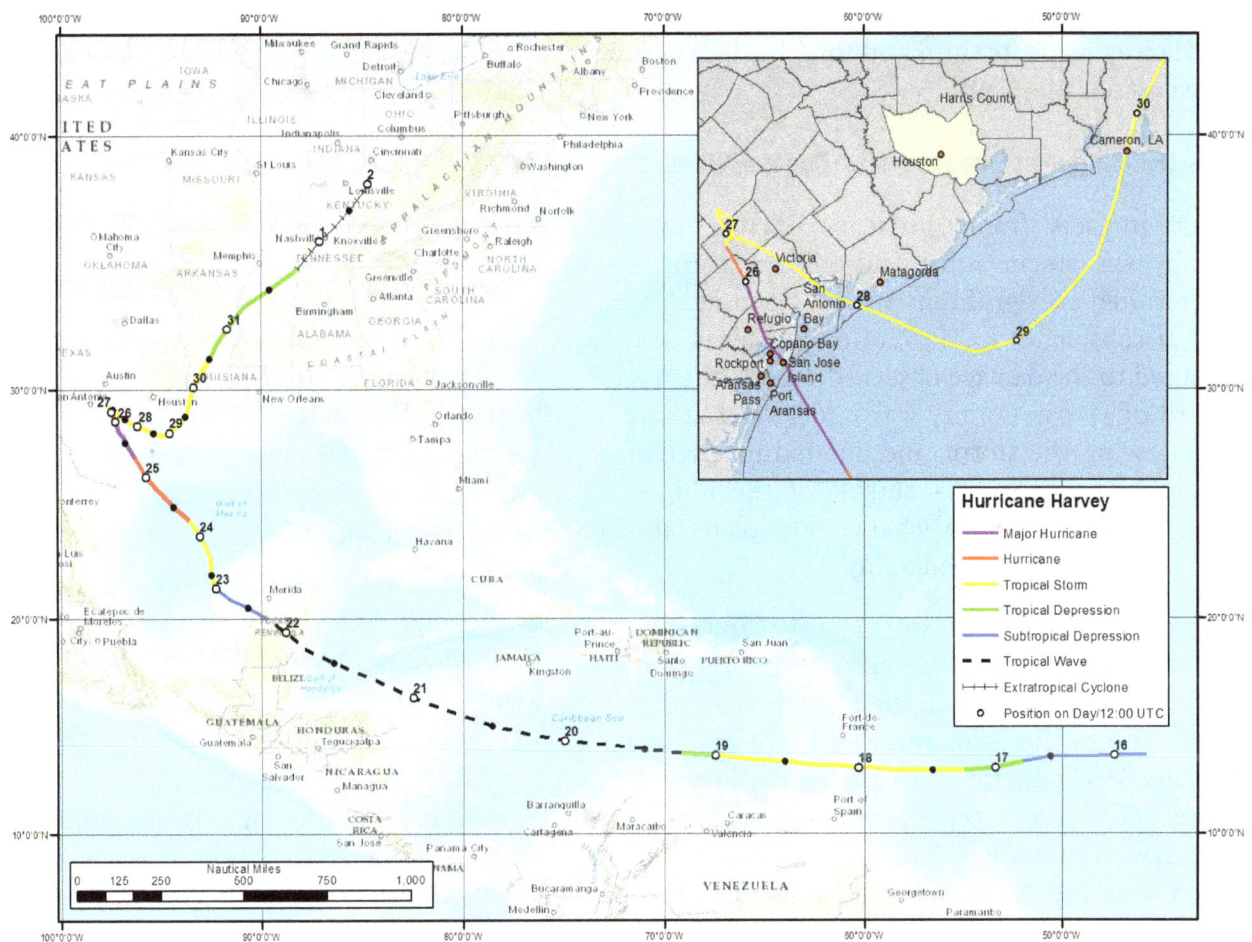

Figure 1-1: Hurricane Harvey Storm Track, August 17, 2017, through September 1, 2017
SOURCE: ADAPTED FROM NOAA NHC, 2018C

Hurricane Harvey made its first landfall in the United States as a Category 4 hurricane over San Jose Island, just north of Port Aransas, Texas, on August 25, 2017, at 10:00 p.m. At landfall, Hurricane Harvey had estimated sustained winds of 130 miles per hour (mph). The storm was approximately 250 miles in diameter, with an eye that was approximately 20 miles in diameter.

Hurricane Harvey's second landfall in the United States occurred three hours later on the Texas mainland, southeast of Refugio, Texas, with estimated sustained winds of 121 mph. Hurricane Harvey continued northwest until the center of the storm stopped northwest of Victoria, Texas. For the next 24 hours, the center of the storm remained almost stationary, making a slow loop that caused bands of heavy rain to continually fall over the Houston metropolitan area and southeastern Texas.

On August 27, 2017, now downgraded to Tropical Storm Harvey, the storm proceeded in an easterly direction, reentering the Gulf of Mexico on August 28, 2017, and slightly strengthening. Tropical Storm Harvey made its third and final landfall on August 30, 2017, near Cameron, Louisiana, with sustained winds of 45 mph.

1.3.1.2 Description of Flood Impacts (Coastal Flooding, Rain, and Sheet Flow)

Flooding impacts from Hurricane Harvey were caused by the storm surge and historic rainfall, which resulted in significant inland flooding. The history of subsidence in Harris County, Texas, also contributed to the damage observed. Approximately one-third of Harris County was underwater at one point following the storm, and approximately half of the inundated area was outside of the FEMA-mapped 0.2-percent-annual-chance floodplain (also known as the 500-year floodplain).

The combined effects of storm surge and tides produced maximum inundation levels of 6 feet to 10 feet above ground level in the coastal counties of Aransas, Nueces, Refugio, and San Patricio. These inundation levels occurred to the north and east of Hurricane Harvey's center in the back bays between Port Aransas and Matagorda, including Copano Bay, Aransas Bay, San Antonio Bay, and Matagorda Bay. Higher inundation levels were recorded near the Aransas National Wildlife Refuge, where high water marks suggested water levels had risen as much as 12 feet.

SUBSIDENCE

Subsidence is the lowering of the ground surface with respect to a fixed elevation and can lead to increased inland flooding along streams and waterways due to changes in stream gradient and ponding near major groundwater extraction areas (e.g., for industrial and drinking water treatment).

Hurricane Harvey was the largest rainfall event in U.S. recorded history. One trillion gallons of rainwater fell in Harris County over a four-day period. The rainfall totals for Hurricane Harvey exceeded the 0.1-percent-annual-chance rainfall (1,000-year event) for many areas in southeast Texas, causing record flood levels for many creeks, rivers, and bayous. In addition to the flooding from riverine sources, sheet-flow flooding damaged thousands of buildings located outside of both the 1.0-percent (100-year event) and 0.2-percent (500-year event) annual chance floodplains by overwhelming stormwater drainage networks, which resulted in stormwater backups. These backups caused rainwater to flow across the ground to the nearest natural drainage, flooding buildings in its path.

During Hurricane Harvey, 14 of the 22 watersheds in Harris County experienced flooding at or exceeding the 0.2-percent-annual-chance levels. An additional seven watersheds experienced flooding at or above the 1.0-percent-annual-chance levels. The severity and extent of the flooding varied significantly between and among the watersheds within the Harris County Flood Control District. For example, while a peak water surface elevation at one gauge on the Buffalo Bayou exceeded the 0.2-percent-annual-chance flood elevation by almost 2 feet, a gauge 20 miles downstream recorded a flood elevation lower than the 1.0-percent-annual-chance elevation.

1.3.1.3 Description of Wind Impacts

At landfall, hurricane-force winds from Hurricane Harvey (i.e., winds of 74 mph or greater) extended 45 miles from the right side and 35 miles from the left side of the storm track.

The wind damage caused by Hurricane Harvey was most severe in the areas where the first two landfalls occurred. In the greater Rockport area, Hurricane Harvey's wind speeds produced pressures that approximated design pressures derived from *Minimum Design Loads and Associated Criteria for Buildings and Other Structures*, American Society of Civil Engineers (ASCE) publication ASCE 7. In Aransas, Nueces, Refugio, and San Patricio Counties, wind forces damaged 40,929 buildings, resulting in $4.58 billion in damage (NOAA NWS Corpus Christi 2018).

1.3.2 Hurricane Irma

1.3.2.1 Formation

Hurricane Irma began as a weak wave of low pressure accompanied by disorganized showers and thunderstorms that emerged off the West African coast on August 27, 2017. The storm progressively strengthened to become a Category 5 hurricane on September 5, 2017, with maximum sustained winds of 185 mph. This made Hurricane Irma one of the strongest observed hurricanes in the open Atlantic Ocean. Figure 1-2 shows Hurricane Irma's track from August 30, 2017, through September 12, 2017.

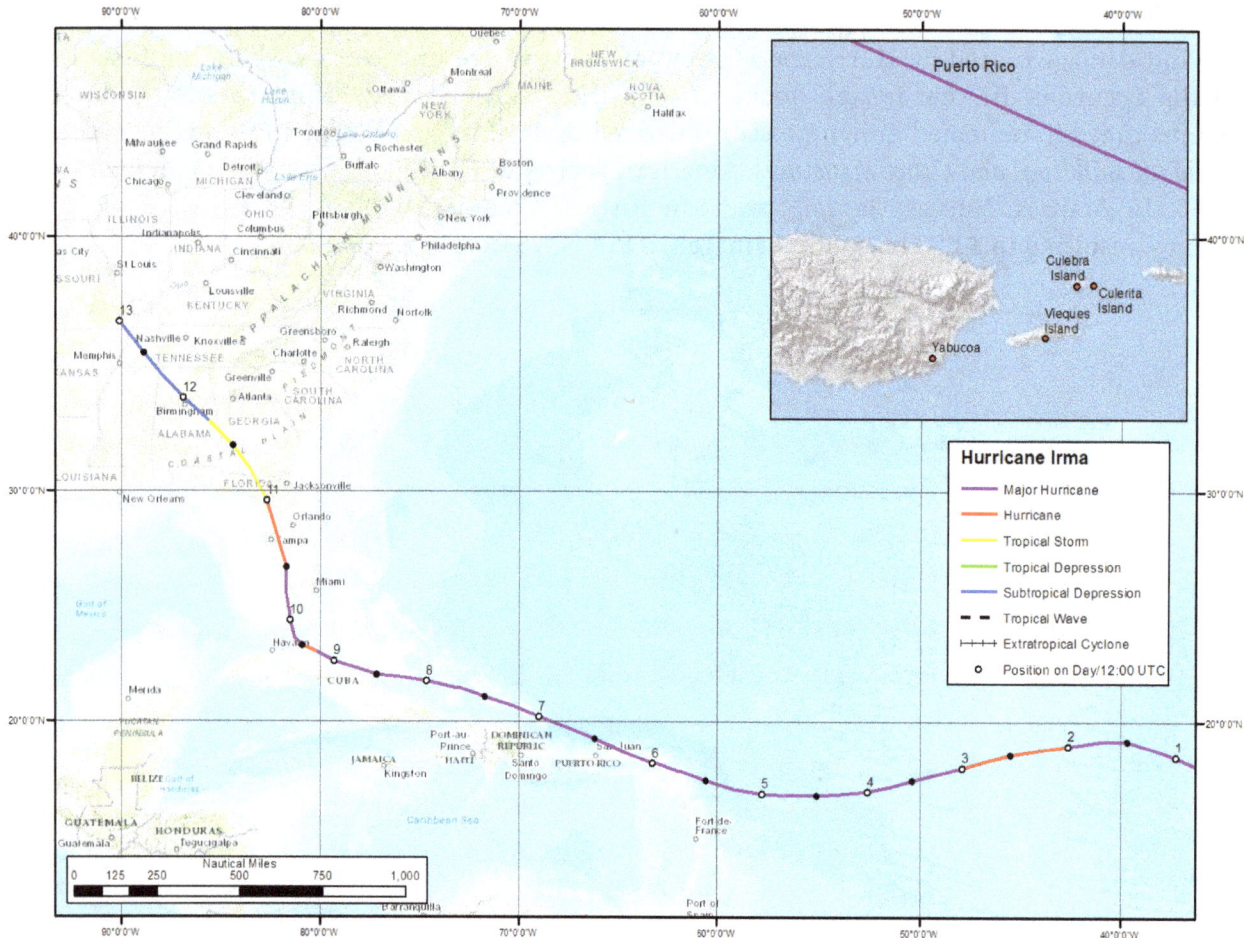

Figure 1-2: Hurricane Irma Storm Track, August 30, 2017, through September 12, 2017
SOURCE: ADAPTED FROM NOAA NHC 2018D

Hurricane Irma made landfall seven times in the northern Caribbean, including four as a Category 5 hurricane. The storm brought strong winds, heavy rain, and, in a few areas, high storm surge, causing widespread devastation across the Caribbean islands and southeastern continental United States.

1.3.2.2 USVI

On September 6, 2017, Hurricane Irma passed over the USVI as a Category 5 storm, with a minimum pressure of 920 millibars (NOAA 2017a). Figure 1-3 shows Hurricane Irma's path through the northern portion of the three islands; the eye of the storm tracked through the British Virgin Islands, northeast of St. Thomas and St. John.

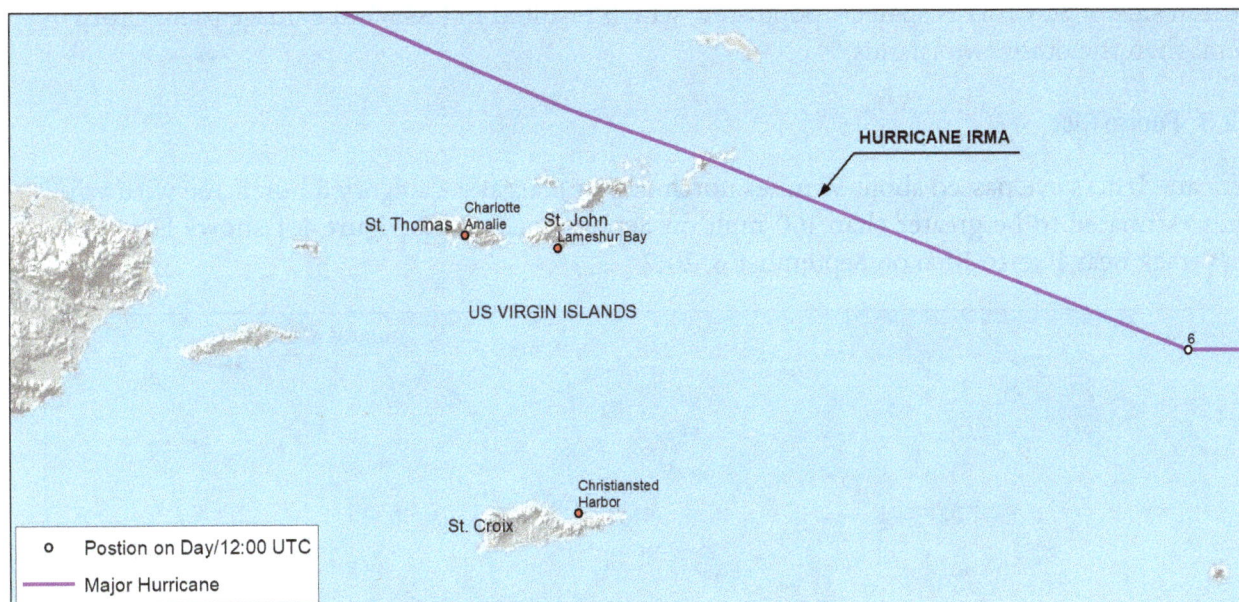

Figure 1-3: Hurricane Irma Storm Track through the USVI on September 6, 2017
SOURCE: ADAPTED FROM NOAA NHC 2018D

Description of Flood Impacts on USVI (Storm Surge and Rain)

Hurricane Irma devastated much of St. Thomas and St. John. The combined effects of storm surge and tide produced maximum inundation levels greater than 2 feet above ground level. The National Oceanic and Atmospheric Administration (NOAA) National Ocean Service (NOS) gauges measured 1.45 feet of storm surge above normal astronomical tide levels in Charlotte Amelie, St. Thomas; 1.62 feet in Lameshur Bay, St. John; and 2.28 feet in Christiansted Harbor, St. Croix (NOAA NHC 2018d). Actual storm surge maximums in St. John are unknown. The NOS tide gauge at Charlotte Amelie did not remain functional during the storm, and other gauges were not located in the most surge-prone areas.

Rainfall across the islands was estimated to be 4 inches to 10 inches from September 6, 2017, to September 9, 2017 (NOAA 2017a).

Description of Wind Impacts on USVI

Both St. Thomas and St. John were significantly impacted by high winds. On both islands, widespread catastrophic damage was reported and trees on the islands were stripped of most of their foliage. Major damage to residential and commercial buildings, critical facilities, and power infrastructure was reported. At the time of landfall in the USVI, hurricane-force winds extended outward up to 50 miles from the eye, with tropical-storm-force winds extending up to 185 miles

(NOAA 2017a). Estimated wind gusts reached approximately 150 mph to 160 mph in St. Thomas and St. John. These speeds were determined from initial modeling using surface-level observations and observed storm pressures (3-second gust at 33 feet for flat, open terrain [ARA/FEMA Geospatial Working Group 2017a]).

Impacts in St. Croix were significantly less due to its southern location and the path of the storm. Although St. Croix was not hit directly by Irma, it still experienced high winds. The mountainous northern side of St. Croix is sparsely populated, which resulted in less wind damage to St. Croix in general than the other two islands.

1.3.2.3 Puerto Rico

Hurricane Irma's eye passed about 57 miles north of San Juan as a Category 5 hurricane with wind speeds estimated to be greater than 160 mph on September 6, 2017. Figure 1-4 shows Hurricane Irma's track near Puerto Rico on September 6, 2017.

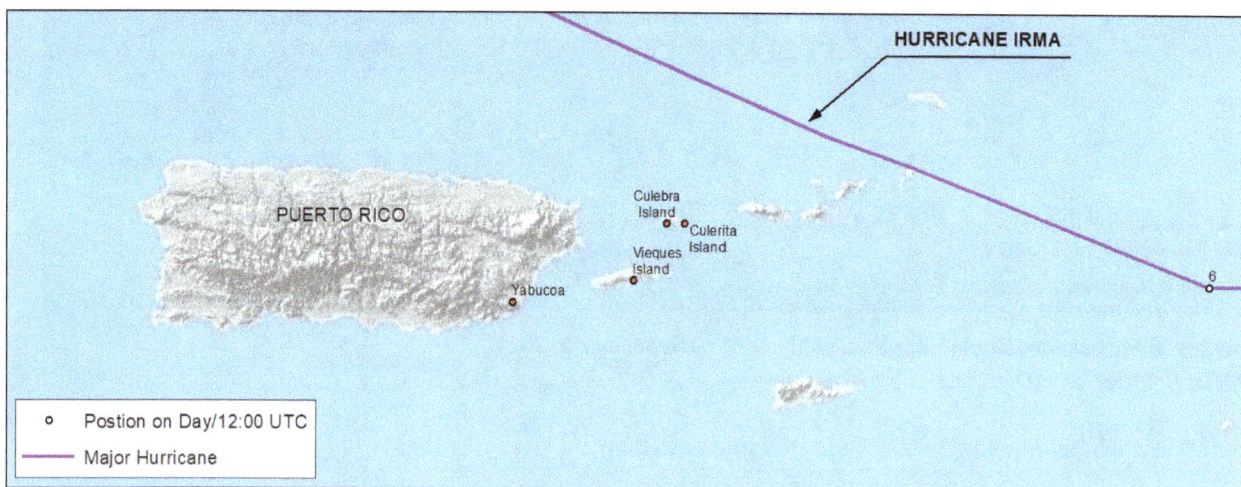

Figure 1-4: Hurricane Irma Storm Track through Puerto Rico on September 6, 2017
SOURCE: ADAPTED FROM NOAA NHC 2018D

Description of Flood Impacts on Puerto Rico (Storm Surge and Rain)

Hurricane Irma caused storm surge flooding in a few areas on the north coast. The deepest inundation was 1 foot to 3 feet above ground level near Arecibo and west of San Juan in Bayamón and Dorado. Buildings on the coast were damaged from storm surge inundation, velocity flooding, and coastal erosion.

Hurricane Irma also produced heavy rainfall in the central and eastern portions of the island, with some higher-elevation areas in the interior of the island of Puerto Rico experiencing 10 inches to 15 inches of rain (NOAA NHC 2018d).

Description of Wind Impacts on Puerto Rico

During Hurricane Irma, the highest wind speeds were experienced on the islands of Culebra and Vieques and along the northeastern coast of the island of Puerto Rico. The highest sustained wind speed recorded in the Commonwealth was 58 mph and a wind gust speed of 89 mph was recorded on the island of Culebra. On the island of Puerto Rico, the highest recorded sustained wind speed was 55 mph, with a gust of 74 mph recorded in San Juan Bay (NOAA NHC 2018d). Many buildings experienced large amounts of water infiltration due to damaged roof coverings, damaged openings (windows and doors) from wind-borne debris, or wind-driven rain entering through unsealed or damaged openings. Damage related to wind speed-up also was noted where groupings of failures occurred in residential settings near larger topographic features.

1.3.2.4 Florida

On September 10, 2017, Hurricane Irma made landfall on Cudjoe Key, Florida as a Category 4 hurricane with maximum wind speeds near 130 mph. As shown in Figure 1-5, the storm made a second and final landfall on Florida's mainland near Marco Island later that day as a Category 3 hurricane with maximum sustained winds of 115 mph before tracking up the Florida Peninsula and into Georgia on September 11, 2017 (NOAA NHC 2018d).

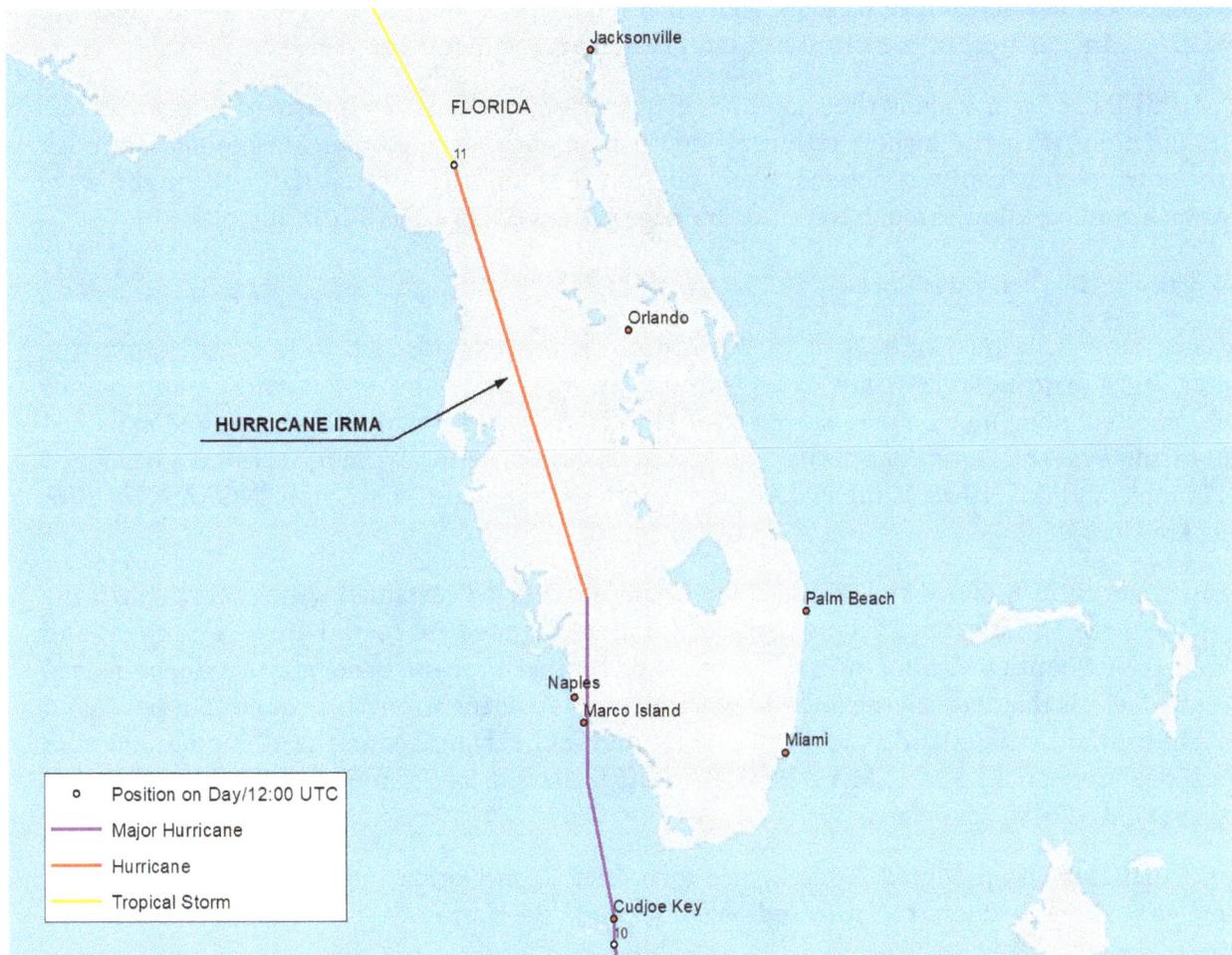

Figure 1-5: Hurricane Irma Storm Track through Florida, September 10, 2017 through September 12, 2017
SOURCE: ADAPTED FROM NOAA NHC 2018D

Description of Flood Impacts in Florida (Storm Surge and Rain)

In addition to the long periods of heavy rain and strong winds, storm surge caused flooding along the Florida coast, particularly on the east side of the state in the Jacksonville area (NOAA NWS 2018). Rainfall totals of 10 inches to 15 inches were common for Hurricane Irma across the peninsula and the Florida Keys. The maximum reported total rainfall for the storm was near the Fort Pierce Water Plant in St. Lucie County, where 21.66 inches of rain was measured between September 9, 2017, and September 12, 2017. Most rivers in northern Florida were flooded, and major or record flood stages were reported at rivers in Alachua, Bradford, Clay, Duval, Flagler, Marion, Nassau, Putnam, and St. Johns Counties.

The combined effect of storm surge and high tides produced maximum inundation levels between 5 feet and 8 feet above ground level for small portions of the Lower Florida Keys from Cudjoe Key eastward to Big Pine Key and Bahia Honda Key. Several high-water marks of at least 4 feet above ground level also were surveyed by the U.S. Geological Survey (USGS) in this area, with the highest mark being 5.45 feet above ground level on Little Torch Key (NOAA NHC 2018d).

In Collier County at Chokoloskee, inundation levels were as high as 6 feet to 8 feet near the waterfront. Inland areas of the island had inundation levels of 3 feet to 5 feet.

In Miami-Dade County along the shoreline of Biscayne Bay, the USGS measured 4 feet to 6 feet of inundation, with the highest estimated depth of more than 5 feet in Matheson Hammock Park. Downtown Miami was flooded, likely due to the combination of rainfall and runoff, wave overwash, and backflow through the city's drainage system (NOAA NHC 2018d).

Description of Wind Impacts in Florida

As Hurricane Irma hit Florida, tropical-storm-force winds extended up to 400 miles from the center, and hurricane-force winds extended outward 80 miles. Sustained hurricane-force winds were reported along much of the east coast of Florida, from Jacksonville to Miami, and extended well inland over the Florida peninsula. The Marco Island Police Department reported a wind gust of 130 mph, and the Naples Municipal Airport reported a wind gust of 142 mph (NOAA NWS 2017; NOAA NHC 2018d).

Many locations in Broward and Miami-Dade Counties reported sustained winds below hurricane force (between 50 mph and 73 mph). Isolated locations (immediate coastal areas of Broward and Miami-Dade Counties within 1 mile of the coast and southern Miami-Dade) may have experienced sustained winds that reached the low end of Category 1 hurricane strength (around 75 mph). Wind gusts in Broward, Miami-Dade, and Palm Beach Counties likely peaked in the 80 mph to 100 mph range. See Section 1.2.3 of FEMA P-2023, *Mitigation Assessment Team Report: Hurricane Irma in Florida* (FEMA 2018c) for details.

Hurricane Irma also produced 25 confirmed tornadoes, 21 in Florida and four in South Carolina. There were three EF-2 (on the Enhanced Fujita Scale), 15 EF-1, and 7 EF-0 tornadoes (NOAA NHC 2018d).

1.3.3 Hurricane Maria

Hurricane Maria originated as a tropical storm on September 16, 2017, approximately 620 miles east of the Lesser Antilles in the Caribbean. By September 19, 2017, Hurricane Maria had tracked northwest toward St. Croix and become a Category 5 storm. Figure 1-6 shows Hurricane Maria's track from September 16, 2017, through September 30, 2017. Hurricane Maria's path cut south of Irma's and directly impacted areas that were spared the worst impacts of Irma two weeks earlier. Figure 1-7 shows a comparison of the tracks of the two storms. Hurricane Irma passed by the USVI on September 6, 2017; Hurricane Maria passed by on September 20, 2017.

In addition to the significant impacts of the storms, the quick succession of storms posed logistical challenges, as relief organizations had staged operations or gathered supplies for Hurricane Irma in places that were now in the path of Hurricane Maria.

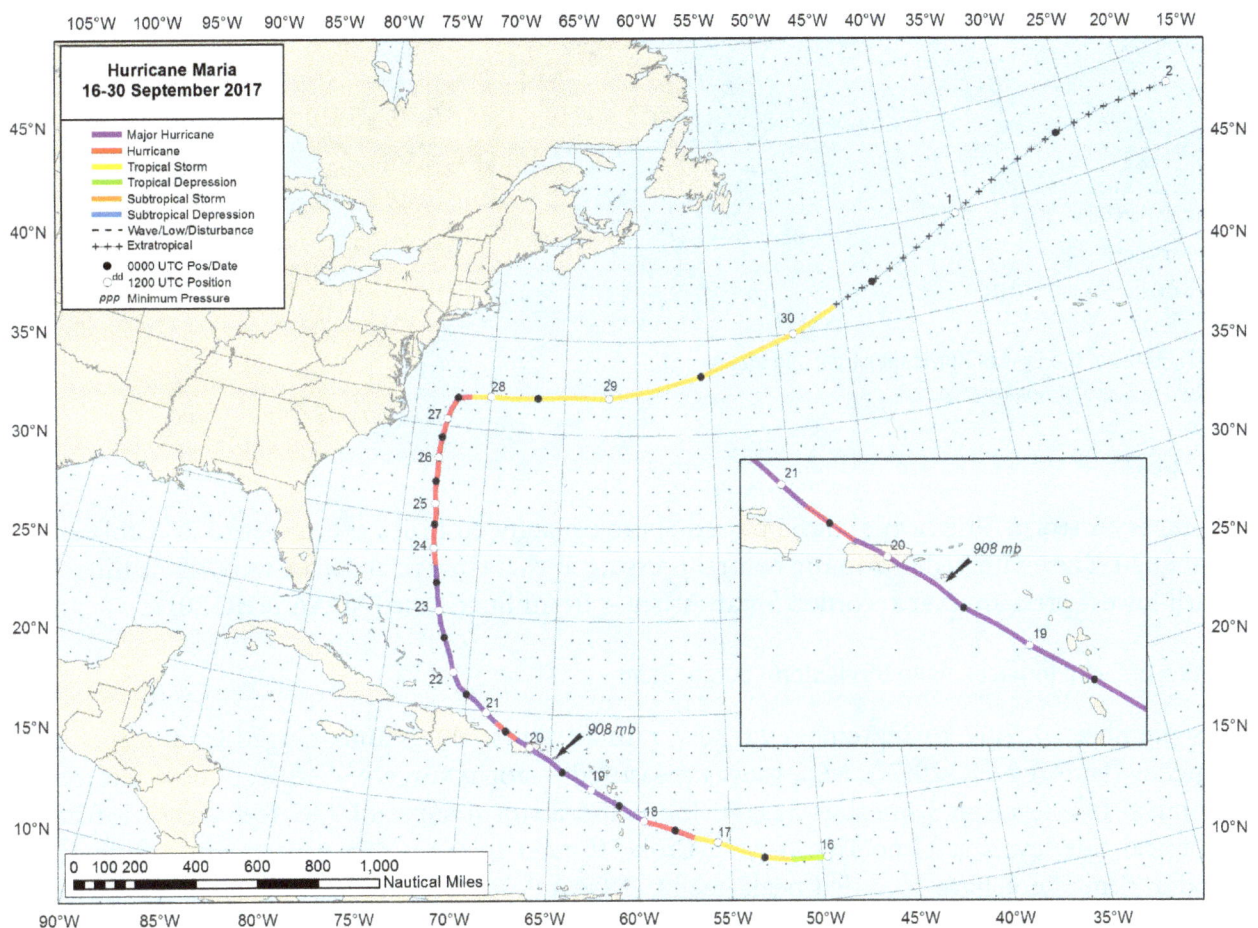

Figure 1-6: Hurricane Maria Storm Track, September 16, 2017, through September 30, 2017
SOURCE: NOAA NHC 2019

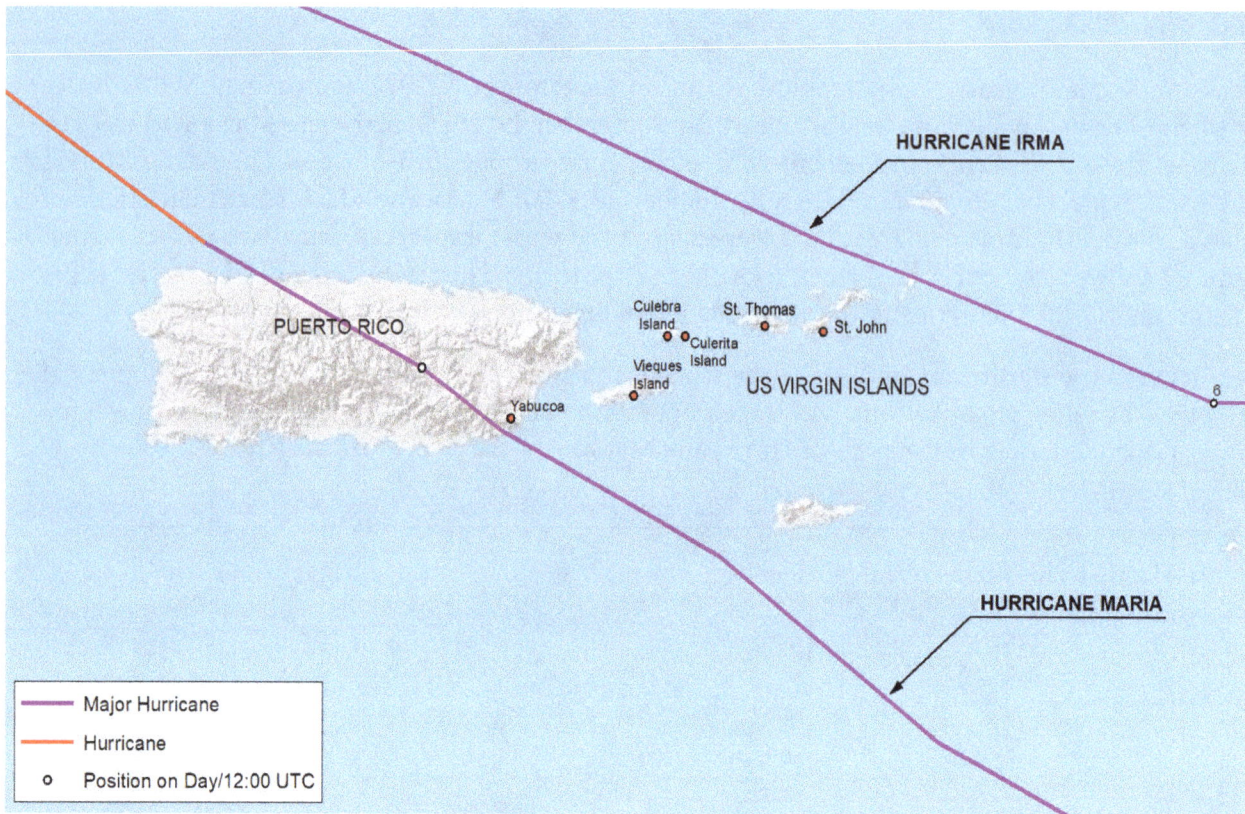

Figure 1-7: Paths of the Eyes of Hurricanes Irma and Maria
SOURCE: NOAA NHC, 2017B, NOAA NHC 2017C

1.3.3.1 USVI

As a Category 5 storm, Hurricane Maria passed approximately 20 miles southwest of St. Croix on September 20. The estimated minimum central pressure at that time in St. Croix was 909 millibars, the tenth lowest pressure ever recorded for an Atlantic Basin hurricane (NOAA NHC 2017d).

Description of Flood Impacts in the USVI (Storm Surge, Rain)

From September 20, 2017, to September 22, 2017, rainfall across the islands ranged from 8 inches to 12 inches (NOAA NHC 2017c). NOS gauges measured a storm surge of 1.48 feet above normal astronomical tide levels at Lameshur Bay, St. John; and a storm surge of 2.85 feet above normal astronomical tide levels at Lime Tree Bay, St. Croix, though the St. Croix gauge went offline for a period and may not have recorded peak height (NOAA NHC 2019). Surge values likely varied substantially across the island because of the storm's location, local topography, and shoreline geometry. Despite potential surge, no notable surge damage was observed by the MAT. As with the previous storm, this was likely due to the relatively steep surrounding continental shelf.

Significant rainfall events also affected the USVI in the month following the storm. Rainfall values of more than an inch each were recorded on October 1, October 9, October 11, and October 27, 2017, in St. Croix (NOAA NHC 2017c). These events further affected damaged buildings that had yet to be suitably repaired. The fact that such events were a further hindrance and possible source of additional damage was considered in the MAT evaluation process.

Description of Wind Impacts in the USVI

Winds generally were strongest along the western and southern portions of St. Croix. Estimated wind gusts up to 140 mph were determined from initial modeling of surface-level observations and observed storm pressures (3-second gust at 33 feet for flat, open terrain, [ARA/FEMA Geospatial Working Group 2017b]).

Hurricane-force winds extended outward 60 miles from the eye of the storm, with tropical-storm-force winds extending up to 150 miles. This meant that St. Thomas and St. John, already recovering from Hurricane Irma, experienced moderate wind speeds.

1.3.3.2 Puerto Rico

Hurricane Maria weakened to a Category 4 storm, but increased in size, before making landfall in Puerto Rico on September 20, 2017, with maximum sustained winds of 155 mph.

Description of Flood Impacts in Puerto Rico (Storm Surge, Rain)

Hurricane Maria caused maximum storm surge inundation of 6 feet to 10 feet above ground level to the east of Maria's landfall along the coasts of Humacao, Naguabo, and Ceiba, as well as the north central municipality of Arecibo. To the southeast, in Yabucoa, Maunabo, Patillas, and Arroyo, maximum storm surge inundation was approximately 4 feet to 7 feet. Along the remaining southern and northeastern coastline, maximum inundation of 3 feet to 5 feet occurred from the municipality of Ponce eastward. The remaining coastline generally experienced inundations ranging from 1 foot to 4 feet. Additionally, the island of Vieques experienced 3 feet to 5 feet of maximum storm surge inundation.

Heavy rainfall occurred throughout the Commonwealth during Hurricane Maria, peaking at 37.9 inches in Caguas. Severe flash flooding occurred in many locations. Thirty rivers reached major flood stage, and 13 of those were at or above previous record stages. Communities along the Guajataca River were displaced when flooding compromised the stability of the dam at Guajataca Lake. Some of the most significant riverine flooding was associated with the La Plata River on the northern part of the island west of San Juan, including the municipality of Toa Baja, where hundreds of people were rescued from rooftops. Landslides associated with the high rainfall occurred throughout Puerto Rico, blocking thousands of roads (Martínez-Sánchez 2018).

Description of Wind Impacts in Puerto Rico

Hurricane Maria's center impacted the southeast coast of Puerto Rico near Yabucoa with maximum winds of more than 150 mph, just below the threshold of Category 5 intensity. The hurricane's center crossed the island diagonally from southeast to northwest, and wind speeds decreased to almost 110 mph. Some of the highest winds were observed on the island of Vieques, southeast of the island of Puerto Rico, and on the island of Culebrita (NOAA NHC 2019).

Hurricane Maria caused lasting interruptions to essential services and severe damage to housing and infrastructure. High winds from both Hurricane Irma and Hurricane Maria contributed to the extensive damage to buildings across Puerto Rico, with hundreds of thousands of homes damaged (Rosselló Nevares 2017). A month after Hurricane Maria, fewer than 8 percent of Puerto Rico's roads were open and usable (Martínez-Sánchez 2018).

1.4 FEMA Mitigation Assessment Team Performance and Data Collection

FEMA conducts building performance studies after unique or nationally significant disasters to better understand how natural and manmade events affect the built environment. A MAT is commonly deployed when FEMA believes the findings and recommendations derived from field observations will result in design and construction guidance that will help improve the disaster resistance and resilience of the built environment.

The MAT studies the adequacy of current building codes and floodplain management regulations, local construction requirements, building practices, and building materials to gain insight about how buildings perform during a disaster.

Lessons learned from MAT observations are communicated through recovery advisories, fact sheets, and comprehensive MAT reports, all of which are made available to communities and the public. Lessons learned can help communities rebuild and design more robust and resilient buildings, structures, and their associated utility systems, thereby minimizing loss of life and injuries, and reducing property damage resulting from future natural hazard events. The accessibility of the MAT materials aids recovery efforts and enhances disaster resilience of buildings and utility systems, whether for existing buildings or new construction. Conclusions and recommendations from MAT reports often are the basis for FEMA's building code proposals and proposed standards and guidance document updates to help improve resilience in design and construction and mitigate damage.

Immediately following each of the 2017 hurricanes, FEMA and building science SMEs conducted desktop analyses of news reports of storm damage, social media, NOAA and Civil Air Patrol photos, and locations of FEMA-funded mitigation projects to identify regions for further observation. FEMA then deployed pre-MAT units to the regions impacted by Hurricanes Harvey, Irma, and Maria to further develop the focus areas for the MATs and identify specific locations for the teams to visit. Specifically, the following MAT teams were assembled and deployed following their respective pre-MATs:

- The Texas MAT deployed after Hurricane Harvey was composed of 27 SMEs divided into four specialty teams: two for flood-related damage and two for wind-related damage.

- The Florida MAT deployed after Hurricane Irma was composed of 17 SMEs divided into two specialty teams: one for flood-related damaged and one for wind-related damage.

■ The Puerto Rico MAT deployed after Hurricanes Irma and Maria was composed of 20 SMEs divided into four specialty teams: building code, permitting, and residential; flood; wind; and support and drone.

■ The USVI MAT deployed after Hurricanes Irma and Maria was composed of 24 SMEs, divided into six specialty teams: building codes, standards, and regulations; residential buildings; schools; hospitals; critical facilities; and solar panels.

MAT members included:

■ FEMA Headquarters and regional staff architects, engineers, and specialists

■ Staff from other federal agencies, including:
  - Department of Defense (DoD)
  - National Institute of Standards and Technology
  - NOAA Sea Grant

■ State and territorial officials

■ Building code, construction, and manufacturing industry specialists

■ Design professionals and technical consultants

■ Insurance company hazard mitigation specialists

MAT member areas of expertise included architecture; structural, civil, coastal, wind, and electrical engineering; emergency management; floodplain management; building codes; construction materials; critical facilities; healthcare; urban floodproofing; and mechanical, electrical, and plumbing (MEP) design and construction.

Full MAT team listings are available in each MAT report. Each MAT team assessed successes and failures to determine why certain buildings performed better than others and what lessons could be learned from each event. To help ensure that consistent information was obtained from each site and keep track of which buildings were visited, the MATs used online tools for data collection or cloud-based data collection applications, where available.

COMPENDIUM REPORT
2017
HURRICANE SEASON

2 Building Codes, Standards, and Regulations

To better understand how buildings were constructed, the MAT reviewed building code histories, floodplain management regulations, and reference standards in the areas impacted by the 2017 hurricanes. Understanding the codes, regulations, and standards helped the MAT identify which building techniques performed well in extreme conditions and which needed improvement.

Model building codes can provide criteria for designers on the minimum loads to which buildings and other structures must be designed to withstand extreme conditions, including minimum elevation requirements for buildings located in flood hazard areas. The most widely adopted building codes in the United States are the International Building Code (IBC) and International Residential Code (IRC), part of a group of codes called the International Codes (I-Codes). The I-Codes are published by the International Code Council (ICC®) and are updated every three years.

In general, buildings observed during the 2017 hurricane season that were built to older codes and standards did not perform as well as those that were compliant with more recent codes and standards and designed to resist flood and wind damage. Additionally, ample evidence suggests that buildings designed to current versions of the IBC and standards that exceed the minimum National Flood Insurance Program (NFIP) requirements are even less likely to sustain damage than those that were not.

2.1 Relationship between Regulations, Building Codes, and Design Standards

The NFIP, floodplain management regulations, building codes, and reference standards all play important roles in the design and construction of buildings to withstand natural hazards. Flood and wind were the primary causes of building damage in the 2017 hurricane season. This section describes the relationship between regulations, building codes, and other design standards as they pertain to flood and wind hazards.

The NFIP is based on the premise that the federal government will make flood insurance available to communities that adopt and enforce floodplain management requirements which meet or exceed the minimum NFIP requirements. The regulations of the NFIP are the basis for local floodplain management ordinances adopted to satisfy the requirements for participation in the NFIP. In addition, the NFIP minimum requirements are the basis for the flood-resistant design and construction requirements in model building codes and standards.

When decisions result in development in Special Flood Hazard Areas (SFHAs), application of NFIP criteria is intended to minimize exposure to floods and flood-related damage. Figure 2-1 illustrates how floodplain management regulations and building codes can be coordinated to fulfil the requirements for participation in the NFIP.

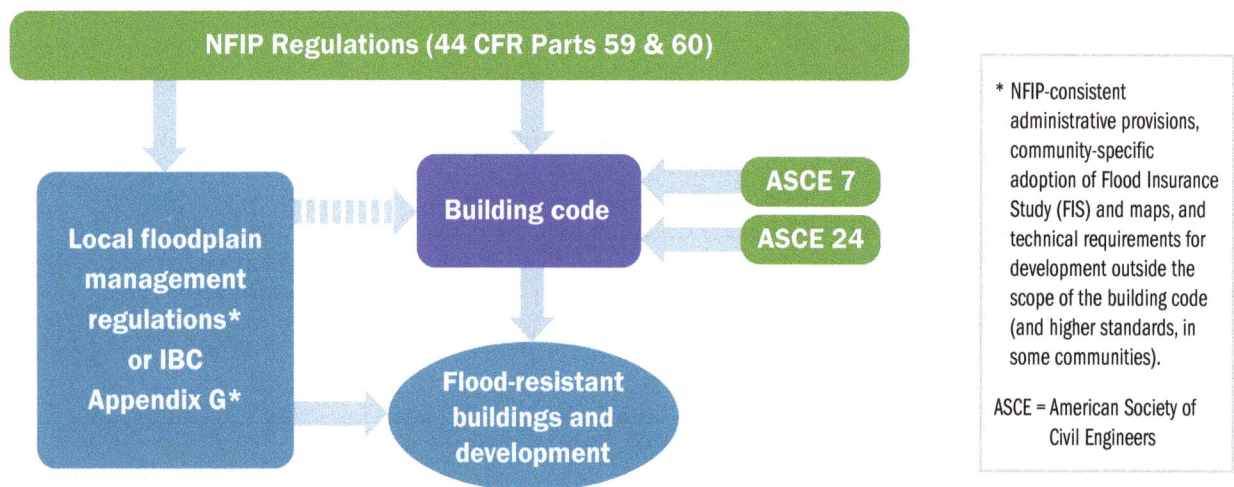

Figure 2-1: Overview of Relationship between Regulations, Building Codes, Design Standards, and Development in Communities with Adopted Codes

The NFIP requirements for buildings and structures are integrated into national consensus standards (ASCE 7, *Minimum Design Loads and Associated Criteria for Buildings and Other Structures* and ASCE 24, *Flood Resistant Design and Construction*) and model building codes such as the I-Codes.

For wind hazards, the design requirements in ASCE 7 are referenced by the model building codes. One key aspect of building design for wind hazards is the design wind speed, which is found in maps in ASCE 7. The design wind speed in the standard is also a function of the assigned risk category. The categories range from I–IV, with I for buildings and structures that represent a low risk to human life in the event of failure; to IV, for critical facilities such as hospitals and emergency operations centers. In the latest version of the standard, separate wind speed maps are provided based on risk category. ASCE 7 also details additional structural design provisions for wind and other hazards, beyond the design wind speed.

Since 1998, FEMA has participated in the code development process for the I-Codes. Every three years, the family of I-Codes is modified through a formal, public-consensus process. The 2018, 2015, 2012, and 2009 editions of the I-Codes contain provisions that meet or exceed the minimum flood-resistant design and construction requirements of the NFIP for buildings and structures. When IBC Appendix G, Flood-Resistant Construction, also is adopted, the minimum requirements for non-building development are satisfied.

For a summary of the NFIP and the minimum requirements for buildings that communities must adopt and enforce to participate in the NFIP, see Section 2.1 of FEMA P-2022, *Mitigation Assessment Team Report: Hurricane Harvey in Texas* (FEMA 2019).

The following sections provide a brief summary of the building codes, standards, and regulations that are specific to each state or territory studied by the 2017 MATs.

2.2 State- or Territory-Specific Building Codes, Standards, and Regulations

2.2.1 Texas

2.2.1.1 Building Code Officials

The state of Texas does not mandate the adoption and enforcement of building codes throughout the state; therefore, municipalities can choose to adopt and enforce any or none of the model building code editions. Those municipalities that elect to adopt codes must, at a minimum, adopt codes from certain editions of the IBC and IRC.

2.2.1.2 Building Code History

Texas has a long history of home rule whereby cities with a population of 5,000 or more may elect a home rule charter, which gives them the authority to enforce building codes and other regulations. Counties and small cities (those with populations of less than 5,000) are restricted to doing only what the state directs or permits them to do. Cities with home rule charters also often have the resources to adopt and enforce building codes, including employment of building code officials, while counties and smaller cities may not.

2.2.1.3 Floodplain Management Requirements

In 2007, the Texas Water Development Board was designated as the NFIP State Coordinating Agency by the State Legislature (Section 16.316, Texas Water Code). The NFIP State Coordinator is the liaison between the federal component of the program and the communities, with the primary duty to provide assistance, guidance, and education for community officials.

Sections 16.3145 and 16.315 of the Texas Water Code give the governing bodies of each city and county the authority to adopt ordinances or orders and "to take all necessary and reasonable actions that are not less stringent than the requirements and criteria" of the NFIP. The state of Texas has no floodplain management requirements established at the state level.

For specific information about the MAT's review of the floodplain management regulations and building codes adopted by Harris County and select cities impacted by Hurricane Harvey, see Section 2.1.3 of FEMA P-2022, *Mitigation Assessment Team Report: Hurricane Harvey in Texas* (FEMA 2019).

2.2.1.4 Wind Requirements

For a summary of the general wind provisions of the I-Codes and referenced standards, see Section 2.2 of FEMA P-2022, *Mitigation Assessment Team Report: Hurricane Harvey in Texas* (FEMA 2019).

Because Texas does not require municipalities to adopt and enforce building codes, the jurisdictions impacted by Hurricane Harvey had adopted different editions of the IBC and IRC, ranging from the 2009 editions to the 2015 editions. However, the Texas Windstorm Inspection Program,

---

ASCE 7 WIND SPEEDS

Because the wind speed definitions and related criteria used in the building codes and standards have undergone two major changes in recent decades, design wind speeds from older codes and standards cannot be directly compared to those in newer versions. ASCE 7 editions prior to 2010 used a service level wind speed, but also included an importance factor and a load factor, which together had the effect of adjusting the return period of the design wind speed from a service level to a strength level. In ASCE 7-10 and subsequent editions, the standard has moved to a strength-level design wind speed (a simplification that eliminated the importance factor and reduced the load factor on wind from 1.6 to 1.0). In addition to other advantages, this change made it easier to compare design wind speeds given in the standard (referred to by ASCE 7 as Basic Wind Speeds) with observed or forecasted hurricane wind speeds. A detailed description of the relationship between wind speeds as defined by ASCE 7 and those in the Saffir-Simpson hurricane wind scale used by the National Hurricane Center is provided in section C26.5.1 of the ASCE 7-16 Commentary (ASCE 2017).

---

through the Texas Department of Insurance (TDI), wields significant influence on construction and building codes in the coastal counties. TDI refers to these counties as "Designated Catastrophe Areas" or "First Tier Counties." TDI requires compliance with the 2006 IBC and IRC with Texas Revisions, which are based on and reference ASCE 7-05 for wind loads.

Texas Windstorm Program

In 1971, as a response to the devastation caused along the Texas coast by previous hurricanes and by Hurricane Celia (1970), the Texas Legislature established the Texas Catastrophe Property Insurance Association (TCPIA) as an insurer of last resort for those unable to obtain windstorm and hail insurance in the private market. The association was renamed and became the Texas Windstorm Insurance Association (TWIA) in 1997. All insurers who provide windstorm insurance in Texas are required to become members of TWIA. Excess premiums and investment income on those premiums are deposited into the Texas Catastrophe Reserve Trust Fund, which is used to pay for excess losses. TWIA operates only in First Tier coastal counties along the 367-mile Texas Gulf Coast.

Texas Department of Insurance

At the same time the TCPIA was established, the Texas Legislature adopted the TCPIA Building Code for Windstorm Resistant Construction, which was based on the wind load provisions of the 1971 Standard Building Code. Various other codes were adopted in later years. Successive hurricanes caused damage that revealed that these code requirements were not being enforced.

This lack of enforcement led to the creation of the Windstorm Inspection Program at the TDI in 1988. The Windstorm Inspection Program currently is responsible for providing product evaluations, construction inspection services, and certification that buildings are in accordance with the adopted codes.

The TDI has adopted various codes for windstorm-related design since the TCPIA was established. For details about the basic tenants of the Texas Windstorm Code, see Section 2.2.3.2 of FEMA P-2022, *Mitigation Assessment Team Report: Hurricane Harvey in Texas* (FEMA 2019).

2.2.2   USVI

2.2.2.1 Building Code Officials

The USVI Department of Buildings, a unit within the Department of Planning and Natural Resources (DPNR), enforces the building and electrical codes, zoning regulations, and other laws, and also is responsible for ensuring the territory meets or exceeds the minimum standards of the NFIP and local ordinances. Further, it is the agency responsible for all building code and regulation enforcement for new construction, repair, or alteration of individual buildings, including those within the SFHA.

The Division of Building Permits within the Department of Buildings is responsible for the enforcement of building codes and regulations and additional administrative tasks.

2.2.2.2 Building Code History

After the unprecedented damage of Hurricane Marilyn in 1995, the USVI government, with the support of FEMA, developed and implemented a new building code. Several years later, FEMA supported DPNR in the crafting of the USVI Building Code (29 U.S. Virgin Islands Code, Chapter 5), which referenced the 2003 I-Codes with amendments that were specific to the Territory.

Amendments included, but were not limited to, requirements for cisterns, island-specific referenced standards, and other local provisions. The code attempted to improve commercial and residential building performance through hazard-resistant construction and, therefore, to minimize wind-borne debris generated by the failure of damaged structures during storms. The legislative adoption of the 2003 I-Codes in the USVI Building Code required the use of anchoring systems, hurricane-resistant metal connectors, and shutters on some buildings.

Code Updates

Through the DPNR Commissioner's interpretation of the USVI Building Code, the Department of Buildings automatically adopts the latest published I-Codes six months after the initial published date. As of March 1, 2018, the Territory adopted the 2018 I-Codes with Territory-specific amendments.

Construction Information for a Stronger Home

The USVI and FEMA developed *Construction Information for a Stronger Home* (the *Stronger Home Guide*) to support natural-hazards-resilient home construction in the USVI. The first edition of this document was published following Hurricane Marilyn and the second in December 1995. The third edition was published in February 1996 and was based upon the 1995 Council of American Building Officials One-and Two-Family Dwelling Code and the 1994 Uniform Building Code.

The *Stronger Home Guide* serves as general guidance and provides prescriptive design measures for residential construction but does not satisfy all building design requirements. (For example, MEP requirements are not covered in the *Stronger Home Guide*.) When using the *Stronger Home Guide*, work must be designed by a registered design professional, along with other requirements. For specific requirements, see Section 2.3 of FEMA P-2021, Mitigation Assessment Team Report: Hurricanes Irma and Maria in the U.S. Virgin Islands (FEMA 2018b).

The fourth edition of the *Stronger Home Guide* (USVI DPNR 2018) was published in 2018 (after the 2017 hurricane season) and references the 2018 IRC, the 2018 IBC, and ASCE 7-16, the latest model building codes and referenced standards, with local input.

2.2.2.3 Floodplain Management Requirements

The current Flood Insurance Rate Maps (FIRMs) for the USVI reference revised maps and data effective April 16, 2007. FEMA has developed Advisory Base Flood Elevation (ABFE) data and other products for the USVI to increase resilience and reduce vulnerabilities within the islands.

2.2.2.4 Wind Requirements

The *Stronger Home Guide* includes general wind design parameters, including for buildings located in certain topographic conditions, an important consideration in the USVI. Topography affects the wind flow around objects, and wind speed is known to increase in areas where hills, mountains, ridges, and escarpments exist, as are found in parts of the USVI. Per the I-Codes, ASCE 7, and the USVI Building Code, the basic design wind speeds near mountainous terrain must be in accordance with local jurisdiction requirements. The local jurisdictions have the option of determining the wind speeds in accordance with Chapter 26 of ASCE 7 or through a wind speed-up model, if one has been developed for their region.

No wind maps showing speed-up effects had been developed for the USVI prior to Hurricane Irma. As a result, design professionals and building officials in the territory had to rely on the procedure provided in ASCE 7 to determine the local effects of wind speed-up for residential construction and renovation.

In response to Hurricanes Irma and Maria, wind speed-up maps were developed for the USVI as part of the MAT effort. The maps can be used as an alternative to ASCE 7 with its own wind speed-up procedures. The new maps simplify the process of incorporating topographic speed-up into design wind speed determinations. For more information about the wind speed-up maps, see Section 2.6 and Appendix E of FEMA P-2021, *Mitigation Assessment Team Report: Hurricanes Irma and Maria in the U.S. Virgin Islands* (FEMA 2018b).

For more information about the USVI wind requirements, see Section 2.3 of FEMA P-2021, *Mitigation Assessment Team Report: Hurricanes Irma and Maria in the U.S. Virgin Islands* (FEMA 2018b).

2.2.3   Puerto Rico

2.2.3.1   Building Code Officials

Development in Puerto Rico is governed by several bodies. The Puerto Rico Planning Board (Junta de Planificación de Puerto Rico, PRPB) guides development. The Permits Management Office (Oficina de Gerencia de Permisos, OGPe) administers building permits and enforces regulations on licensing, inspections, certification, and land use planning. Autonomous municipalities across Puerto Rico also may be granted degrees of fiscal autonomy and self-government if they meet certain requirements.

PRPB

In May 1942, the PRPB was created by Law No. 213 to regulate development in the Commonwealth through systematized and organized planning. (PRPB Audit and Compliance Bureau 2017). Today, the PRPB continues to guide development to meet current and future needs (PRPB 2010). It acts as an extension of the Governor "… to design and formulate the short, medium, and long-term public policy of economic development, and the use of the resources of the Island" (PRPB 2017). The PRPB regulates construction and prepares maps of geographic limits of Puerto Rico municipalities and neighborhoods. In April 2017, the PRPB also was granted authority to carry out compliance inspections and audits of permits granted by OGPe and the 17 permit offices of the autonomous municipalities (PRPB Audit and Compliance Bureau 2017).

OGPe

In December 2009, OGPe was created by Act No. 161 to implement a new and more efficient permit system. OGPe replaced the Regulation and Permitting Administration (Administración de Reglamentos y Permisos, ARPE), which had previously governed the permitting process in Puerto Rico since its establishment in 1975.

OGPe enforces regulations, including those on land use planning, licensing, inspections, certification, and permitting. OGPe also serves a unifying, coordinating role to enforce permitting regulations developed by PRPB (PRPB Audit and Compliance Bureau 2017).

OGPe handles permitting and inspections from a main office in San Juan and regional offices in Aguadilla, Arecibo, Humacao, and Ponce. Municipal officials have identified this as problematic, because staffing and office locations limit OGPe's ability to inspect every project.

Autonomous Municipalities

Law No. 81 of 1991, or the Autonomous Municipalities Act of 1991, is an extraconstitutional Puerto Rican law that regulates the local government of all the municipalities of Puerto Rico. The law allows municipalities to have degrees of fiscal autonomy and self-government at a local level. Section 13.012 of this Act defines five tiers of delegation of authority. Autonomous municipalities are those at the highest tier, Tier 5, which have a Land Ordination Plan in effect. Tier 5 autonomous municipalities may acquire powers for regulating construction that are otherwise reserved for the PRPB and OGPe. Delegation of planning authority to a municipality requires that the municipality establish a Permits Office and have a territorial plan in effect, among other requirements. The Act may set limitations to the delegated powers according to the municipality's capacity.

2.2.3.2 Building Code History

The 2011 Puerto Rico Building Code (PRBC), adopted in March 2011, was in effect at the time of the 2017 hurricanes and is based on the 2009 I-Codes. Local amendments included a municipality-based map for IBC, "1613.5 Seismic Ground Motion," that used the most conservative ground acceleration within the municipality. For the IRC, a local amendment to "R301.2.12 Protection of Openings" expanded the design wind speed allowance for prescriptive-based wood structural panels for wind-borne debris region opening protection from 130 mph to 145 mph. This is a significant amendment, as all of Puerto Rico is within the 145-mph design wind speed for the 2011 PRBC.

In November 2018, Puerto Rico adopted a new building code based on the 2018 I-Codes with no amendments weakening natural-hazard-resistant provisions of the model codes. In addition, six amendments recommended by the Puerto Rico MAT were adopted:

- Clarification of the requirement to update to the latest I-Codes and consensus standards on a three-year cycle

- Requirement of territory-wide corrosion protection for vulnerable building elements

- Requirement of SFHA documentation for replicable building design submittals. (This requirement resulted in two separate amendments to ensure proper inclusion in applicable provisions of the code)

- Requirement of storm shelters for schools (defined as Group E occupancy in the IBC)

- Requirement of storm shelters for critical facilities

For details about the code history of Puerto Rico, see Section 2.1 of FEMA P-2020, *Mitigation Assessment Team Report: Hurricanes Irma and Maria in Puerto Rico* (FEMA 2018a).

2.2.3.3 Floodplain Management Requirements

Puerto Rico has participated in the NFIP since 1978. Development is governed by Puerto Rico's floodplain management ordinance, Planning Regulation 13, effective January 7, 2010. Building permits within the floodplain are the responsibility of OGPe. Puerto Rico has five NFIP communities that may adopt and enforce floodplain management regulations. These five NFIP communities encompass all 78 of the municipalities of Puerto Rico. The largest community is the Commonwealth of Puerto Rico, which includes 74 municipalities. The additional NFIP communities are the municipalities of Bayamón, Carolina, Guaynabo, and Ponce.

Planning Regulation 13 enacted NFIP-compliant standards for floodplain management, including the requirement of a minimum of one foot of freeboard for residential structures. There is no freeboard requirement for non-residential structures under Planning Regulation 13.

Ponce is the only community in Puerto Rico that participates in the Community Rating System (CRS). Ponce is a Class 9 community under the CRS rating system, which entitles residents in SFHAs to a 5-percent discount on their flood insurance premiums. The MAT observed interest in the CRS from other municipal officials who wished to lower the cost of flood insurance.

The 2018 I-Codes include a number of floodplain management provisions that have changed since Regulation 13 was issued in 2010. The two documents currently are not consistent. For example, Planning Regulation 13 has no freeboard requirement for commercial structures; however,

> **COMMUNITY RATING SYSTEM**
>
> The Community Rating System (CRS) is a program developed by FEMA to provide incentives for those communities in the NFIP that have gone beyond the minimum floodplain management requirements to develop extra measures to provide protection from flooding. Policy holders in communities that participate in the CRS may qualify for reduced NFIP insurance premiums for exceeding minimum requirements. For more information about the CRS program, please visit https://www.fema.gov/national-flood-insurance-program-community-rating-system.

2018 IBC, which references ASCE 24-14, requires a minimum of 1 foot of freeboard for commercial structures; more than 1 foot may be required, depending on the building's Flood Design Class. Refer to *Highlights of ASCE 24 Flood Resistant Design and Construction* (FEMA 2015b) https://www.fema.gov/media-library/assets/documents/14983 for more information.

2.2.3.4 Wind Requirements

Design wind speeds for Puerto Rico can be found on maps in ASCE 7. During the 2017 hurricane season, the code in place in Puerto Rico referenced ASCE 7-05, which designates a basic wind speed of 145 mph island-wide. Wind speeds for different Risk Categories are accounted for indirectly through the importance factor. For more information about the wind requirements for Puerto Rico during the 2017 hurricane season, see Section 2.4 of FEMA P-2020, *Mitigation Assessment Team Report: Hurricanes Irma and Maria in Puerto Rico* (FEMA 2018a). The 2018 PRBC (adopted after the 2017 hurricane season) references ASCE 7-16 and includes new micro-zoned design wind speed maps, which include the effects of topographic wind speed-up.

2.2.3.5 Solar Equipment

In Puerto Rico, the permitting of photovoltaic (PV) panels is managed by OGPe, not the municipalities. Approval by the Puerto Rico Electric Power Authority (Autoridad de Energía Eléctrica, PREPA), is required for the system to be connected to the electric grid. Permitting of solar power and heating systems is covered under general building requirements, which call for a permit to be certified by a design professional for projects costing more than $6,000. According to municipal officials, PV systems typically go through the permitting process regardless of their cost, because PREPA requires a permit showing the installation is code-compliant. Conversely, installation of a solar water heater on existing buildings typically falls below the $6,000 threshold for a certified permit. The solar water heater installation does not need PREPA review; therefore, solar water heater installations typically are unpermitted according to municipal officials.

Puerto Rico added an amendment to the IBC that includes design pressures for components and cladding where solar water heaters and PV panels are mentioned. This is the only specific design guidance for solar equipment wind speeds or pressures given in the 2011 PRBC and its reference standards, including ASCE 7-05.

Other references to solar equipment appear in the PRBC for installation processes; however, these references are broad and focus primarily on the condition of the installation components. Another amendment included in the 2011 PRBC includes a requirement that all new houses and townhouses use only solar water heaters. Specific design guidelines are not provided. This lack of guidance is especially noteworthy given that local permitting does not review or inspect PV panels or solar heating system installations. Chapter 6 of FEMA P-2020, *Mitigation Assessment Team Report: Hurricanes Irma and Maria in Puerto Rico* (FEMA 2018a), details the performance of ground-mounted PV systems and residential and non-residential rooftop solar equipment.

2.2.3.6 Safe Room Requirements

While the 2011 PRBC does not mandate the construction of storm shelters or safe rooms, Puerto Rico has approved an amendment to the 2018 PRBC that requires schools and critical facilities to provide storm shelters.

2.2.4 Florida

2.2.4.1 Building Code Officials

The Florida Building Code (FBC) is maintained and updated by the Florida Building Commission with administrative support and technical assistance from the Florida Department of Business and Professional Regulation. Although the FBC is required to be updated every three years, the Commission may revise the code annually to incorporate Declaratory Statements (interpretations), clarifications, and standard updates.

2.2.4.2 Building Code History

The FBC is part of the Florida Administrative Code adopted through Rulemaking as governed by Chapter 120 of the Florida Statutes. The adoption of the FBC by the Florida Building Commission as a Rule is mandated by the Florida Legislature (the code is not adopted statutorily).

Local jurisdictions in Florida are permitted to amend the FBC, provided such amendments do not weaken the code. As part of the triennial code development process, the state's Commission reviews local amendments for consideration and inclusion in the FBC. However, the Commission does not have authority to approve or disapprove local amendments.

Local amendments expire with the effective date of each new edition of the codes, which means communities must re-adopt local amendments every three years. The most common technical amendments related to the wind provisions of the code clarify the specific location of the wind speed contours.

When Hurricane Irma made landfall in Florida on September 10, 2017, the 5th Edition (2014) FBC was in effect. The 5th Edition (2014) FBC is based on the 2012 Edition of the applicable I-Codes published by the ICC. The base codes are revised by Florida-specific amendments through Florida's code development process to create the FBC.

The 6th Edition (2017) FBC was adopted on June 13, 2017, although Rulemaking had an effective date of December 31, 2017. The 6th Edition (2017) FBC is based on the applicable 2015 I-Codes.

For a detailed summary of the Florida code adoption history, see Chapter 2 of FEMA P-2023, *Mitigation Assessment Team Report: Hurricane Irma in Florida* (FEMA 2018c).

2.2.4.3 Floodplain Management Requirements

Many Florida communities, through local floodplain management regulations, have adopted and enforced provisions that exceed the NFIP minimum requirements for buildings. A statutory provision was added in 2010 specifically for local amendments to the FBC flood provisions.

Under three circumstances in the statute, these amendments do not expire every three years as other local amendments do: (1) if they are locally adopted before July 1, 2010; (2) if the higher standard is freeboard; and (3) if the higher standard is adopted for the purpose of participating in the NFIP CRS.

For a detailed summary of floodplain management in Florida, see Section 2.2 of FEMA P-2023, *Mitigation Assessment Team Report: Hurricane Irma in Florida* (FEMA 2018c).

2.2.4.4 Wind Requirements

The design of buildings for wind loads in Florida is governed primarily by the Florida Building Code, Building (FBCB); the Florida Building Code, Residential (FBCR); and the Florida Building Code, Existing Building (FBCEB). The 5th and 6th Editions of the FBC reference the 2010 Edition of ASCE Standard 7, *Minimum Design Loads for Buildings and Other Structures* (ASCE 7-10). However, the FBCB, FBCR, and FBCEB also contain numerous Florida-specific, wind-related amendments that exceed the minimum criteria in the I-Codes.

The FBC also contains separate wind, structural, and testing requirements for a special zone called the High-Velocity Hurricane Zone (HVHZ). The HVHZ, specifically defined as Miami-Dade and Broward Counties, was created for the inaugural version of the FBC (2001) as a way to maintain certain wind-related provisions from the South Florida Building Code. The wind criteria applicable in the HVHZ historically have been more stringent than the criteria applied in the rest of the state. However, more recent versions of the code have been minimizing the differences.

For a detailed summary of the wind provisions of the FBC, see Section 2.3 of FEMA P-2023, *Mitigation Assessment Team Report: Hurricane Irma in Florida* (FEMA 2018c).

2.2.4.5 Manufactured Home Requirements

The Florida Department of Highway Safety and Motor Vehicles has jurisdiction over the installation of Manufactured Housing Units (MHUs). Requirements for installation, setup, tie-downs, and anchoring foundations, with specific provisions related to wind loads, are contained in Chapter 15C of the Florida Administrative Code. With respect to installation in flood-prone areas, the regulations refer to and incorporate by reference the 1985 edition of FEMA 85, *Manufactured Home Installation in Flood Hazard Areas*.

COMPENDIUM REPORT
2017
HURRICANE SEASON

3 Building Performance

The MATs observed damage to buildings, building equipment, and associated structures caused primarily by flooding and high winds from the three hurricanes. While observing building-related damages, the MATs also inspected certain building performance issues in detail. This chapter is structured to present flood and wind hazard damages, as well as the impacts of these damages on different building types.

The first two sections of this chapter provide a general discussion of the damages observed due to flood and wind hazards. The third section discusses the implications of poor performance for the various types of buildings observed by the MATs during the 2017 hurricane season.

3.1   Flood Hazard Observations

The following sections describe key flood hazard-related observations from the MATs. Chapter 4 includes tables with conclusions and recommendations related to flood hazard observations.

3.1.1   Flood Damage Outside the Regulatory Floodplain

The MAT teams observed that flood damage to buildings was not limited to properties in mapped 1.0-percent-annual-chance probability floodplains. In Harris County, TX, aerial imagery revealed that about one-third of the county was under water at one point, and approximately half of the inundated area was outside of the FEMA-mapped 0.2-percent-annual-chance probability floodplain, thus outside the SFHA. Many non-elevated or low-elevation buildings with floors at or near adjacent grade sustained flood damage.

The Puerto Rico MAT observed many areas not located in designated flood zones that are nevertheless at high risk of localized flooding. These locations are susceptible to flooding due to runoff from local terrain, poor building siting, or poor local drainage. Additionally, many buildings in mountainous regions are at risk from landslides in heavy rains. Many buildings sited on steep slopes were observed to be at risk of collapse from landslides triggered by flooding.

The USVI MAT observed many locations in which low-lying areas experienced flooding because of ponding water that lacked sufficient drainage to transport water away from buildings after heavy rainfall. Many residents of the USVI experienced water infiltration into homes after water spilled over roadways and onto residential property. Unlike most identified flooding from riverine or coastal sources, flooding from stormwater runoff is currently not shown on FIRMs.

3.1.2   Residential Buildings

Residential building performance in flood conditions varied across the states and territories. Most of the inland flooding observed during the 2017 hurricane season occurred in Texas, whereas coastal flooding damage was observed in Florida and Puerto Rico. The MAT teams in the USVI observed little flood damage likely due to the steep nature of the surrounding continental shelf and the inland location of many buildings. This section highlights the key building performance observations for residential buildings.

3.1.2.1   Elevation

The MATs observed that elevation of residential structures was a good predictor of building performance relative to flood hazards. Buildings constructed at or near grade were subject to deeper and more damaging flooding. This applied to buildings subject to storm surge and to buildings subject to rainfall-induced flooding. The Texas MAT visited select residential buildings (primarily single-family dwellings) that were flooded by Hurricane Harvey in Aransas, Harris, and Nueces Counties. Building elevation was a universal indicator of performance: many older buildings built before communities joined the NFIP and began regulating SFHA development were inundated 3 feet to 6 feet deep, while newer elevated residential buildings performed much better, in some cases with no inundation and other cases with less than 1 foot of flooding above the lowest floor. In buildings that had been elevated, the Texas MAT observed that compliance with floodplain management requirements for enclosures below elevated buildings was inconsistent. The MAT observed structures with an insufficient number of openings, as well as structures with openings that did not meet requirements (e.g., improperly sized).

3.1.2.2 Slope Stability, Erosion, and Scour

Siting was an important factor in building performance in Florida during Hurricane Irma, and in Puerto Rico during Hurricanes Irma and Maria. The Florida and Puerto Rico MATs observed many cases of erosion and scour, along with variable performance of erosion control structures (Figure 3-1).

The Puerto Rico MAT observed many residential buildings that were spared from significant damage during Hurricanes Irma or Maria but lost their ocean-facing decks to storm-induced erosion. The team also observed many protective walls damaged by Hurricane Maria, leaving the loose ground beneath them susceptible to erosion. Many coastal buildings observed by the Puerto Rico MAT were not identified as being in a coastal flood hazard area on the existing FIRMs, so were not required to be built to withstand coastal erosion impacts.

Figure 3-1: Undermined houses constructed on top of the dune in Vilano Beach, FL.

These houses survived the undermining, even though approximately 10 to 15 feet of dune height was lost beneath the houses. The pilings farther seaward are for a seawall under construction at the time of the MAT visit (February 2018).

The Puerto Rico MAT also observed many residential and low-rise buildings located in inland areas where the topography was very steep and mountainous. Many of the buildings were either carved into the natural slope of the existing hillside or placed on fill materials used to build up the outside edge of the existing hillside. These homes are at very high risk of damage or destruction because they are extremely vulnerable to erosion, landslides, and other slope stability hazards.

3.1.2.3 Flood-Damage-Resistant Materials

Perimeter wall foundations (crawlspaces) were observed in many of the newer elevated homes in Texas. Crawlspaces must have flood openings to allow the equalization of flood forces. One common performance issue observed by the MAT was the use of non-flood-damage-resistant materials in crawlspaces, particularly insulation. Use of such materials requires an additional factor of safety be incorporated into the foundation design flood elevation, or freeboard, to reduce the risk of damage.

Conversely, the concrete and concrete-framed buildings common in Puerto Rico performed better than wood-framed buildings under most inland flood and rainfall conditions. This was because most concrete buildings in Puerto Rico used either uninsulated concrete or concrete masonry unit (CMU) infill walls, both of which are included in NFIP Technical Bulletin 2, *Flood Damage Resistant Material Requirements* (FEMA 2008).

3.1.3 Non-Residential Buildings with Dry Floodproofing

Due to the flooding caused by Hurricanes Harvey and Irma in Texas and Florida, MAT teams in these states conducted detailed evaluations of dry floodproofing in non-residential buildings. In Texas, many of the buildings where dry floodproofing measures were implemented had experienced flooding damage during Tropical Storm Allison in 2001. In general, the teams observed that dry floodproofing measures often failed under less-than-design conditions. This section discusses several of the key observations made by the teams.

3.1.3.1 Failures and Near Misses

The MATs observed several dry floodproofing systems that either failed or came very close to failing during Hurricanes Harvey and Irma. In these cases, the dry floodproofing measures or human intervention prevented widespread flood damage, but if flood levels had been only slightly higher or if building managers had not acted before the onset of flooding, many of these successes would have been failures.

Dry floodproofing systems were observed to fail for reasons including unsealed penetrations in the walls of floodproofed buildings; lack of gaskets, failure of gaskets due to physical damage or degradation over time, gasket compression during storage, leaking valves (air gasket systems); or lack of substantially impermeable walls, use of non-flood-damage-resistant materials, and failure to maintain the integrity of the flood barrier. One example of a failure was at a historic building in Miami, FL, where the system failed, causing approximately 3 feet of flooding in part of the building. The MAT observed unsealed penetrations in the historic walls and air gaskets that had deflated.

One example of a near miss was the City of Houston's Department of Public Works building. The building is in an Unshaded Zone X, approximately 600 feet from the nearest regulated floodplain. Like many buildings in Houston, the Public Works building flooded during Tropical Storm Allison because of the tunnel network flooding, which connects many of the downtown buildings. Following Tropical Storm Allison, a 74-inch partial height flood door was installed in the parking garage that connects to the Public Works building and the tunnel network. During Hurricane Harvey, floodwaters reached 70.75 inches, nearly overtopping the 74-inch-high door. While this door performed well and was not overtopped, there was no redundancy to prevent catastrophic damages from occurring had the flooding exceeded 74 inches.

3.1.3.2 Implementation Considerations

If building managers or staff must be actively involved in initiating a dry floodproofing measure, it is important that they be prepared to do so. The MAT teams observed dry floodproofing systems with implementation processes ranging from those that could be easily deployed by two workers in less than two hours to those that would take several workers multiple days to implement.

SUCCESS STORY:
Texas Medical Center,
The University of Texas MD Anderson Cancer Center

The buildings that make up the MD Anderson Cancer Center are located in Shaded Zone X or Zone AE; their Base Flood Elevations (BFEs) vary, depending on their location. The Cancer Center dry floodproofing measures include a complete perimeter floodwall with active and passive floodgates, sump pumps, flood doors in the basement, elevation of utilities and backup generators, and a continuous flood monitoring system. In addition, the Cancer Center's management has instilled a culture of preparedness, including regularly scheduled exercises.

During Hurricane Harvey, none of the buildings in the Cancer Center lost utility service or the ability to provide patient care. The Cancer Center did not evacuate or turn away any patients. The northern campus of the Cancer Center was cut off by floodwater for slightly more than two days. Portions of the main building were surrounded by three feet of water in the streets, but floodwater never rose high enough to threaten the building or flood barriers. There was one point of failure when a manhole cover blew off on the dry side of the floodwall, causing minor flooding in the lobby area. Overall, the hurricane caused minimal impacts to the facility. This was a result of thorough and well-executed plans, a culture of preparedness among staff, independent testing of the dry floodproofing measures, and other mitigation measures implemented by the Cancer Center.

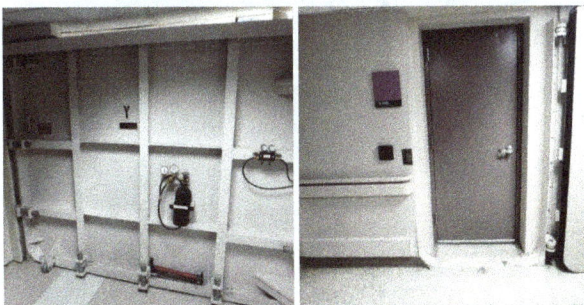

Flood doors in basement that subdivide basement areas within the main building.

Buildings that survived with minimal damage generally had building managers who instilled a culture of preparedness and ensured redundancy. These managers held regular training and exercises to ensure that staff knew how to properly deploy floodproofing systems in the event of a flood. On the other hand, MATs also observed flood protection components not stored in a dedicated or secure location, making it difficult to deploy these protective components efficiently or effectively, and difficult to ensure that all components are accounted for. In many cases, the implementation of dry floodproofing measures was handled by contractors, so building owners and managers may not understand how to operate the systems.

3.1.3.3 Operations and Maintenance

Most of the buildings visited had emergency operations plans, including plans describing how to implement dry floodproofing measures. Some plans, however, did not include all relevant information to ensure successful implementation of the dry floodproofing measures. The MAT teams observed that it was important to ensure continuity across staffing changes to ensure that knowledge of how to operate floodproofing systems is not lost to staff turnover. Building managers should design emergency operations and maintenance plans that meet the requirements in Chapter 6 of ASCE 24, to improve dry floodproofing system deployment. Additional guidance on maintaining and deploying dry floodproofing systems, as well as on developing emergency operations and maintenance plans that meet the requirements of Chapter 6 of ASCE 24, could improve dry floodproofing system deployment.

3.2 Wind Hazard Observations

The following sections describe key wind hazard-related observations from the MATs. Chapter 4 includes tables with conclusions and recommendations related to wind hazard observations.

3.2.1 Topographic Effects on Wind Speeds

The Puerto Rico MAT observed that many residential and other low-rise buildings constructed along hillsides and on hilltops of mountainous terrain experienced increased wind forces during Hurricanes Irma and Maria. Hurricane winds are channeled through mountainous terrain. As the wind moves over hills, ridges, bluffs, escarpments, and up mountain valleys, the wind speeds often increase as the topography rises. The effect is much like how the speed of water in a pipe increases when a nozzle constricts the flow. The MAT observed damage caused by this speed-up effect at abrupt changes in topography, such as the upper one-half of hills, ridges, and escarpments. Figure 3-2 demonstrates the impacts of wind speed-up on three similarly constructed homes. The black areas on the roofs are areas where the roof covering was missing. The variation in damage likely was caused due to wind speed-up.

In severe cases, topographic wind speed-up on buildings can cause significant damage or catastrophic failure. While the MAT observed potential instances of this, the teams were not able to confirm the quantitative contribution of wind speed-ups to these observed building failures.

New map products were developed for the USVI and Puerto Rico that incorporate the effects of terrain on wind speeds. See Section 2.2.2.4 and Section 2.2.3.4 for more information.

Figure 3-2: Roof damage from wind speed-up effects

These homes are located in Palmas del Mar in Humaco along the eastern coastline.

3.2.2 Structural Systems / Main Wind Force Resisting Systems

> **MAIN WIND FORCE RESISTING SYSTEM (MWFRS)**
>
> MWFRS is defined in ASCE 7-16 as the "assemblage of structural elements assigned to provide support and stability of the overall building" (ASCE 7-16).

The primary determinant for retaining the structural integrity of a building is the proper design and installation of the structural or Main Wind Force Resisting System (MWFRS). Much of the observed MWFRS performance against wind hazards during the 2017 hurricane season was for residential structures. This section describes the unique observations in residential structures across the four states and territories visited by the MATs, as well as the performance of manufactured homes. This section is organized by location as each location had unique performance observations depending on storm conditions and/or local building codes.

3.2.2.1 USVI

Hurricane Marilyn (1995) damaged or destroyed approximately 21,000 homes in the USVI. Most of the damage occurred on St. Thomas and was caused by blow-off of the roof structure and/or roof covering. The findings from analysis of this widespread damage provided the basis for the residential roof designs provided in *Construction Information for a Stronger Home* (the *Stronger Home Guide*) (USVI DPNR 1996). In addition, FEMA funded roof repairs on a subset of damaged buildings through the Home Protection Roofing Program (HPRP) following Hurricane Marilyn.

In the wake of Hurricanes Irma and Maria, the MATs assessed HPRP homes and homes constructed according to updated building codes and/or the *Stronger Home Guide*, as well as homes constructed before Hurricane Marilyn and not retrofitted, to compare structural performance.

HOME PROTECTION ROOFING PROGRAM

Following widespread damage to homes after Hurricane Marilyn, FEMA provided technical assistance and funding for repairing or replacing roofs for approximately 350 homes in the USVI through the Home Protection Roofing Program (HPRP). One of the key components of the HPRP was to address the issue of poorly attached roofs that could be blown off during hurricanes. FEMA collaborated with local USVI officials to develop two HPRP design solutions: improving the attachment of corrugated metal roof panels and building roofs by applying a liquid-applied membrane over plywood. Both options included design solutions for improving the wind resistance of the joists or beams. The HPRP either replaced or upgraded a home's entire roof assembly, including the roof structure, regardless of the level of damage. Through FEMA's Hazard Mitigation Grant Program, funding was granted to the USVI, providing the Territory with resources for design, construction, formal construction management oversight, and quality assurance and quality control.

HPRP Homes

The USVI MAT found that roofs on buildings that participated in the HPRP program generally performed well during Hurricanes Irma and Maria. The HPRP homes typically had low-sloped gable or hipped wood-framed roofs built over an existing structure. The roof extended to the edge of the supporting wall face, where an extremely short eave remained almost flush with the building and this design was able to resist high winds. Generally, the number and strength of connections were substantial, as the load path from roof covering to sheathing to roof structure to wall carried the wind loads adequately. The shallow slopes, lack of overhangs, and consistent strength of connections likely mitigated any potential wind damage. The fascia board and edge finishes were rarely damaged on HPRP homes and potentially helped brace the roof sheathing to the roof structure near edges. Proper layering of these elements also allowed for further sealing against wind-driven rain and rain overflow from gutters.

The majority of HPRP roofs used corrugated metal panels readily available throughout the islands. These roofs were sometimes treated with a liquid-applied coating that added a further layer of waterproofing to the metal surface. Other HPRP homes used a liquid-applied roof membrane directly on the wood panel sheathing. This type of roof membrane system has less likelihood of wind uplift due to the integrated nature of the design.

Non-HPRP Homes

Structural and roof performance varied on non-HPRP homes depending on whether the home had been constructed in accordance with the post-Marilyn building codes or the guidelines in the *Stronger Home Guide*. The homes that had MWFRS damage appeared to be those constructed prior to Hurricane Marilyn, or if constructed post Hurricane Marilyn, they did not comply with the post-Marilyn building code changes. Figure 3-3 shows damage to a house on St. Thomas that was typical of many homes constructed prior to Hurricane Marilyn, with structural steel roof frames and light-gage purlins. The MAT also observed traditional CMU homes with wood-framed roof structures that suffered significant damage due to high winds. In one observed case, a home lost most of the roof structure facing the peak hurricane winds. These traditional CMU homes sometimes experienced wall damage as well, often at the top of walls near damaged rooflines.

Figure 3-3: Typical home constructed before Hurricane Marilyn

Homes in USVI constructed before Hurricane Marilyn typically can suffer blow-off of a steel roof structure

On non-HPRP homes that performed well in the hurricanes, the most common roof types were corrugated metal panels (Figure 3-4) and liquid-applied membranes (Figure 3-5). Systems that appeared to have been constructed in accordance with the *Stronger Home Guide* generally performed well. The common exception was roofs with external gutters. This type of gutter design was frequently blown off in high winds during the storms.

Figure 3-4: A corrugated metal panel roof with integral gutter.

This home appeared to comply with the Stronger Home Guide.

Figure 3-5: A liquid-applied membrane over plywood with wood battens roof system.

This roof system and integral gutter appeared to comply with the Stronger Home Guide.

Homes in the large Sion Farm neighborhood at the center of St. Croix typically were partially pre-fabricated concrete structures and performed well during Hurricanes Irma and Maria, although the winds from these events did not directly strike the island. These homes had flat roofs constructed of the same pre-cast reinforced concrete panels as the walls and foundation. The roofs and reinforced pre-cast wall panels of these homes (Figure 3-6) performed well and did not sustain structural damage from the storm. These homes maintained their building envelopes and were strong enough to repel windborne debris. In some cases, small leaks occurred in places where the roofline sagged from settling and inadequate rooftop drainage.

Figure 3-6: Typical Sion Farm home constructed of pre-cast concrete wall and roof panels.

These buildings and their concrete roofs performed very well in response to wind loads. Sion Farm neighborhood, St. Croix.

3.2.2.2 Texas

The Texas MAT observed wind-related MWFRS failures, including roof and wall structure failures. The team observed that roof systems of residential buildings were particularly vulnerable to the high winds of Hurricane Harvey, but that damage varied across the areas visited. Positive wind pressures under roof eaves and large overhangs and roof surfaces caused significant damage to many homes.

Connectors and sheathing are critical elements of the MWFRS. Structures in coastal high-wind zones should have robust MWFRS connections to adequately transfer loads from the roof structure to the wall structure and into the foundation's system. Figure 3-7 shows an older home whose roof structure failed due to poor connections of the rafters to the joists.

Figure 3-7: Older home with roof failure in Rockport, TX

In addition to robust connectors, another vital part of the MWFRS is the sheathing—both roof and wall sheathing. Roof sheathing transfers roof loads to the rafters and trusses. Wall sheathing in a shear wall transfers lateral loads to the wall system, which transfers the loads to the foundation. To perform as intended, sheathing must be rated for its purpose and installed properly with fasteners that are installed according to the building code and manufacturer's recommendations.

3.2.2.3 Puerto Rico

Residential Construction

Residential construction in Puerto Rico is commonly described as either "formal" or "informal." Formal construction follows adopted building codes and standardized practices. It is officially permitted either by OGPe or by an autonomous municipality. Formal construction is overseen by, and requires final approval from, a professional engineer or registered architect. In contrast, informal construction is "self-built" without proper permitting and without design professional supervision during the construction process. Informal construction may be non-compliant with building code, zoning, or title requirements. In general, the prevalence of informal construction is a major challenge to the effective implementation and enforcement of building codes.

"Approximately 50 percent of Puerto Rico's housing units are informal or have uncertain legal standing." (Resilient Puerto Rico Commission 2018). Reasons for the existence of informal construction prior to Hurricanes Irma and Maria included a lack of adequate resources to enforce and remediate unpermitted construction and OGPe's current exemption from design professional certification requirements for certain projects costing less than $6,000 (PRPB n.d.).

> **LOAD PATH OBSERVATIONS**
>
> Observations of proper load paths were used to distinguish informal from code-compliant construction. This typically was possible for wood-framed buildings but not possible with only visual observations for most concrete and CMU buildings.

Following Hurricanes Irma and Maria, Administrative Order 2017-07 was issued on October 5, 2017 (OGPe 2017) to encourage rapid reconstruction, but it also may have served to perpetuate the prevalence of informal construction. It enabled certain aspects of reconstruction, replacement, or repairs to commence without the requirement of a government-issued permit.

Structural Performance

The most common structural failures in Puerto Rico were partial failures of the MWFRS and failures of components and cladding systems. The MAT observed that reinforced concrete and CMU homes with concrete roof decks performed best under wind loads, as these homes typically were professionally designed and permitted and constructed with sufficient strength to withstand the wind forces.

Additions to existing houses were frequently wood-framed construction. These additions were commonly second stories atop a concrete or CMU home or additions to the side of the home. Most of these additions were informally constructed, with little to no engineering design, and these structures performed poorly, with loss of roof covering, roof structure (no deck was present), and wall failures.

In addition to one- and two-family dwellings, the MAT visited low-rise buildings used for multi-family residential and light commercial use. In general, these buildings had a continuous load path that resisted wind loads without failure, as they were likely formal construction and thus designed and constructed to resist these loads. Exceptions to this good performance occurred when building materials were in poor condition or where the building was impacted by falling or wind-borne debris.

3.2.2.4 Florida

Wind damage to roof structures often was found to have initiated through loss of the roof covering or breaching of the attic envelope, though the cause of the initial failure could not always be determined after the event. After wind enters a building, failures can progress to other components and connections along numerous load paths. Framed walls of residential structures collapsed where significant portions of the roof and ceiling diaphragm were destroyed by wind and the lateral support for the walls was compromised.

> **STAGED CONSTRUCTION**
>
> It is common practice in Puerto Rico and the USVI to build homes with steel reinforcing bars protruding through the roof, so that the homeowner may add an upper floor in the future. The MAT observed such staged construction practices throughout Puerto Rico and the USVI. However, steel rebar that is left unprotected for months or years can corrode and weaken, making it unsuitable for its intended use.

An example of wall failure in Florida was observed on Ramrod Key, as shown in Figure 3-8. The two story, wood-framed residence (built in 1990) lost roof trusses above the east-facing (ocean-facing) second floor area; two exterior walls were lost from the room below the missing roof trusses, and the adjacent deck floor collapsed onto the porch floor below.

Although failures of the MWFRS were observed in some buildings, most buildings designed and constructed to comply with the FBC performed well. However, many of these same buildings sustained wind-induced failures of building envelope components that allowed wind-driven rain to enter, resulting in costly damage. Building envelope damage is discussed in Section 3.2.3.

Figure 3-8: House with wind damage.

Roof structure loss and collapse of the second-floor exterior wall and adjacent deck.

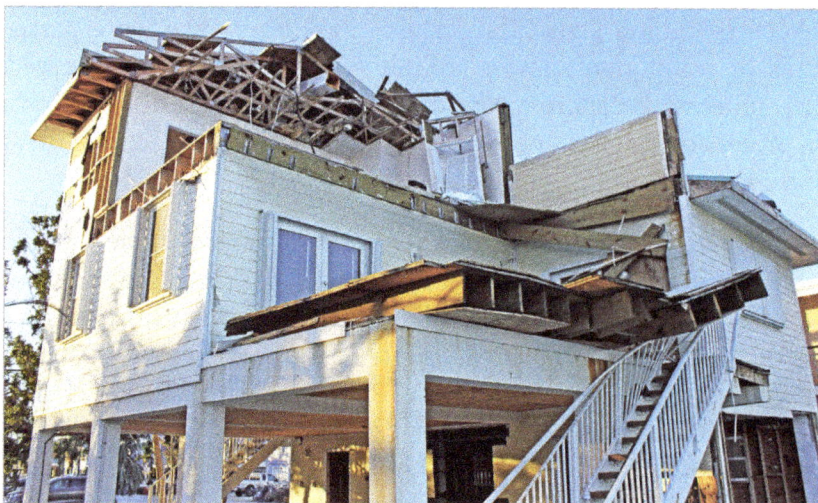

3.2.2.5 Manufactured Housing

Historically, MHUs have performed poorly under hurricane-force wind loads, wind-driven rain, and wind-borne debris. After Hurricanes Irma and Maria, the Florida and USVI MATs observed MHUs that experienced near-total damage from wind events that were at or below design levels.

USVI

After Hurricanes Irma and Maria, the USVI MAT visited two neighborhoods on St. Croix containing MHUs. Several of the homes sustained severe damage and were effectively destroyed beyond repair. One such home lost roofing and siding, exposing the interior of the wall finish to heavy rains. The roof, siding, and wall sheathing were all blown off the home and many of the windows were broken by debris.

Although new MHUs are no longer allowed to be deployed to USVI, the MAT observed that existing units often were repaired even after sustaining significant damage. Interior and exterior labels and plates often were removed during renovations or after being damaged, so the MAT had difficulty identifying the age and design criteria used for many of the MHUs observed.

Florida

The Florida MAT observed MHUs in Collier County and the Florida Keys after Hurricane Irma. The MAT report focused primarily on units in Collier County, as many of the MHU installations in the Florida Keys were destroyed by storm surge. The Collier County MHUs suffered wind damage, as described. Aside from newly installed units, the MAT observed significant variation across MHU installations with respect to the spacing of anchors and where they were connected to the unit. Figure 3-9 illustrates typical anchorage variations observed in older installations. Loose anchor straps also were commonplace. Without adequate tension, the anchor straps are ineffective at resisting the lateral and uplift effects of high wind.

Figure 3-9: MHU installation with wind damage.

On this MHU installation, only the first and fourth straps are attached to the exterior wall base.

Yellow circles show where straps are attached to the base of the unit wall. The inset shows close-up of loose strap inside red outline.

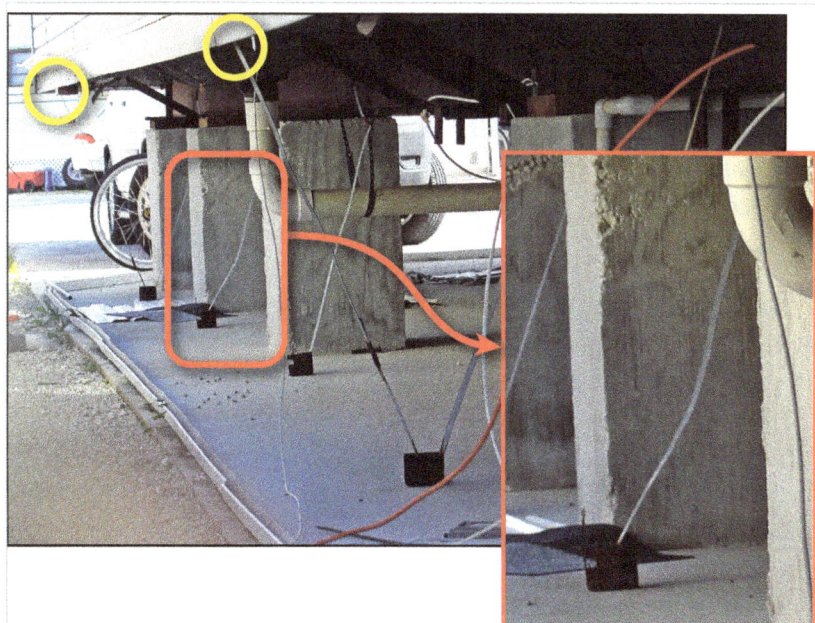

Wind damage to MHUs frequently is initiated when improperly attached appurtenances are blown off or damaged. Specifically, when carports and covered porches—which are particularly vulnerable to wind loads—break away from the MHU, they leave openings at failed connections in the remaining roof and/or wall that allow wind and rain to enter the MHU envelope. In some cases, damage progresses from the initial point of failure. The MAT observations confirm this progressive failure pattern occurred in Florida during Hurricane Irma.

3.2.3   Building Envelope

This section describes common damage observed in various elements of the building envelope.

3.2.3.1   Openings

Windows and doors (glazed, open / louvered window assemblies, and rolling doors) are vulnerable to damage and failure from wind pressures, water intrusion, and wind-borne debris. Damage to windows, doors, and other openings allows wind-driven rain to enter through and around existing openings and can result in significant damage to the building and contents.

All four of the MATs observed many types of openings (glazed windows, open / louvered window assembles, sectional garage doors, and others) that failed under wind pressures or impacts from wind-borne debris, leaving structures vulnerable to internal wind pressures, wind-driven rain, or other damage. Table 4-12 in the next chapter presents the MAT conclusions and recommendations related to the performance of openings.

Many of the homes the Texas MAT observed, and some homes in the USVI and Puerto Rico, had windows that were protected by impact-resistant shutters in lieu of impact-resistant glazing, plywood shutter installations, and many types of removable and operable shuttering systems, including classic fixed-in-place overhead coiling shutters. In general, these impact-resistant shutters performed well.

JALOUSIE WINDOWS

Jalousie windows are the most common window system observed in residential buildings in Puerto Rico and the USVI. Jalousie window systems contain panels (louvers) made of metal, glass, or wood that typically are opened or closed by turning a handle to allow natural ventilation to help control the temperature inside the building while limiting sunlight into the building and providing visual privacy. Because they are inherently "open," non-sealed systems, they allow the passage of wind-driven rain, water, and air into buildings. Wind pressures allowed in through jalousie windows can overload the roof and cause failure. The common use of metal panel jalousie window systems in informally constructed homes contributed to the failure of many roof systems in the residential buildings the MAT observed. The photo above shows a close-up of a jalousie window with metal lovers on a residential building in Puerto Rico.

Impact-resistant shutters cannot prevent water intrusion through jalousie windows, however, which are inherently unable to prevent water from seeping between their operable louvers.

In Florida, the FBC defines wind-borne debris regions, within which the code requires protection of all exterior glazed openings with products meeting the Large Missile Test of ASTM E 1886 and ASTM E 1996, Testing Application Standards 201, 202, and 203 (HVHZ Test Protocols), AAMA 506, or ANSI / DASMA 115 (garage doors). However, the few instances where the Florida MAT observed damage to protected glazed openings occurred in areas where estimated wind speeds during Hurricane Irma were well below the 130 mph wind-borne debris trigger for which glazed opening protection is required. For details of the MAT observations, see Section 4.2.4 of FEMA P-2023, *Mitigation Assessment Team Report: Hurricane Irma in Florida* (FEMA 2018c).

The Texas MAT observed many sectional garage doors that were not rated for high winds that failed during Hurricane Harvey. The USVI MAT observed large, overhead roll-up doors at critical facilities that failed under wind loading and debris impact. Very few hurricane-rated sectional doors were observed to have failed.

> **SUCCESS STORY**
>
> The fire stations visited by the Puerto Rico MAT had been equipped with hazard-resistant shutters with HMA funding in 2001. Later, a number of public buildings received wind retrofits, including shutters, following Hurricane Irene in 2011. Shutter performance was successful in every case the Puerto Rico MAT observed when shutters were fully deployed.
>
> In one case, some shutters were not in place at the time of the event, allowing windows to be damaged by wind-borne debris. This damage illustrates the need for an adequate operations and maintenance plan and execution of the plan.

3.2.3.2 Roof Coverings

Damage to roof coverings is one of the leading causes of building performance issues during hurricanes. A damaged roof covering allows rainwater to enter the building, which can cause extensive and costly damage to the interior finishes and contents.

Residential Roof Coverings

There was widespread residential roof covering damage throughout Puerto Rico. The typical failure points of roof coverings were from insufficient attachment of the roof covering to the roof structure (in the absence of a roof deck) or inadequate attachment to the roof decking. Many wood-framed roofs were damaged due to inadequate roof covering or attachment.

In Florida, asphalt shingle loss was observed to be widespread, especially in the Florida Keys. Asphalt shingle failure was observed on older dwellings and those built after adoption of the FBC. Older asphalt shingle roofs on pre-FBC dwellings were more vulnerable to wind damage than newer roofs on post-FBC buildings. Residential metal roof systems performed well overall, with a few isolated instances of damage. The damage to metal roof systems that the MAT observed generally was limited to roof edges.

In Texas, the MAT observed varying degrees of damage across roof coverings, including asphalt shingles, architectural standing seam metal panels, and various types of cementitious clay tiles.

See Section 3.2.2.1 for information about the performance of roof coverings in USVI.

Non-Residential Roof Coverings

Damage to USVI hospital facilities was due primarily to wind forces and wind-driven rain that damaged one or more elements of the building envelope. While some roof covering remained in place during the storms, several roofs experienced partial or complete roof covering blow-off.

A variety of school roof coverings were observed in the USVI, including metal panels, liquid-applied membranes over concrete roof decks, and single-ply and modified bituminous membranes. Metal panels included exposed-fastener systems (corrugated metal panels and R-panels) and standing-seam panels with concealed clips. In many instances, corrugated roof panels were not attached securely or in accordance with recommended guidance. Significant corrosion of corrugated panels was observed at some schools. The MAT observed that membrane roofs were not blown off but were commonly punctured by wind-borne debris.

The Texas MAT observed roof covering failure at an older medical center with a built-up roof. Aggregate from built-up roofs may become wind-borne debris, impacting unprotected glazing and injuring patients seeking treatment at the hospital. A large portion of this roof membrane blew off during Hurricane Harvey, initiated by the lifting of the top nailer flashing to which the gutter was attached in some locations, and gutter uplift in others (Figure 3-10).

The impacts of rooftop equipment on non-residential roof coverings is described in Section 3.2.4.

Figure 3-10: View of emergency repairs

At this older medical center, the roof above the emergency room area needed emergency repair work. The red arrow indicates a section of metal edge flashing that blew onto the roof.

3.2.3.3 Exterior Wall Coverings

This section summarizes observations about exterior wall covering (also known as cladding or siding) performance, including brick veneer and vinyl siding. In both Texas and Florida, the MATs observed that residential wall coverings had inadequate resistance to wind pressures. This caused widespread loss of these coverings, which sometimes served as an initiation point for progressive failure and the entry of wind-driven rain.

Brick Veneer

During Hurricane Harvey, seaward and inland zones in Texas experienced at or near ASCE 7-05 and TDI hurricane design wind speeds. Numerous brick veneer failures throughout the Hurricane Harvey damaged areas were observed, on residential and non-residential buildings alike. Many of the residential brick veneer structures observed by the MAT to have suffered damage from Hurricane Harvey were older residential structures and apartments, but some newer mid-rise condominiums also suffered significant masonry cladding failures. The observed performance was reflective of these higher wind speeds, but, more importantly, showed the lack of adherence to good installation practices. Common failure modes include tie (anchor) fastener pull-out due to failure of masons to embed ties into the mortar, poor bonding between ties and mortar and mortar of poor quality, randomly spaced brick ties, and tie corrosion.

Vinyl Siding

The MAT observed exterior wall covering damage and loss resulting from Hurricane Irma in Florida. Aside from a few isolated instances of damage to wood siding, most of the exterior wall covering damage observed by the MAT was to vinyl siding. Damage to vinyl siding was observed to be widespread in the Florida Keys and also was observed in Collier County. In most cases, the Hurricane Irma MAT could not determine the design pressure rating of the failed vinyl siding. However, most of the observations indicated that the failed vinyl siding did not appear to be rated for high-wind regions. The text box that follows on the next page describes the difference between high-wind and standard vinyl siding.

In a few homes, the MAT was able to record product identification numbers that allowed them to compare product-specific wind ratings to the FBC requirements and wind speeds experienced during Hurricane Irma.

Comparing the observed pressure rating to the design requirements for one home that lost siding in Sugarloaf Key, the siding should have resisted wind pressures sustained during Hurricane Irma. In another home in Marathon Key, a comparison of the pressure rating on the installed siding revealed that it was 27 percent less than the required design pressure. However, based on the estimated wind speeds at the site, the siding should have resisted wind pressures experienced during Hurricane Irma if it was properly installed.

3.2.3.4 Soffits

The MAT observed widespread damage to soffits in the Florida Keys, particularly vinyl soffits. Wind-damaged soffits allowed wind-driven rain to enter building envelopes, resulting in costly damage to building interiors. MAT wind observations of soffit loss are grouped according to common material types present in South Florida: vinyl and metal (aluminum and steel). In some

HIGH WIND-RATED VINYL SIDING VS. STANDARD VINYL SIDING

Much of the failed vinyl siding that the Irma MAT observed in Florida did not appear to be rated for high-wind regions. Technical Fact Sheet 5.3, "Siding Installation in High-Wind Regions," in FEMA P-499, *Homebuilders Guide to Coastal Construction* (2010), includes guidance on vinyl siding installation. The left-side graphic below from Technical Fact Sheet 5.3 demonstrates the basic differences between vinyl siding rated for high-wind regions and standard vinyl siding. The right-side image is siding from one of the damaged houses in Goodland. Note how the detached siding has a standard (single) hem and locking area depicted in the left image (rather than the high-wind siding required by the FBC in the area).

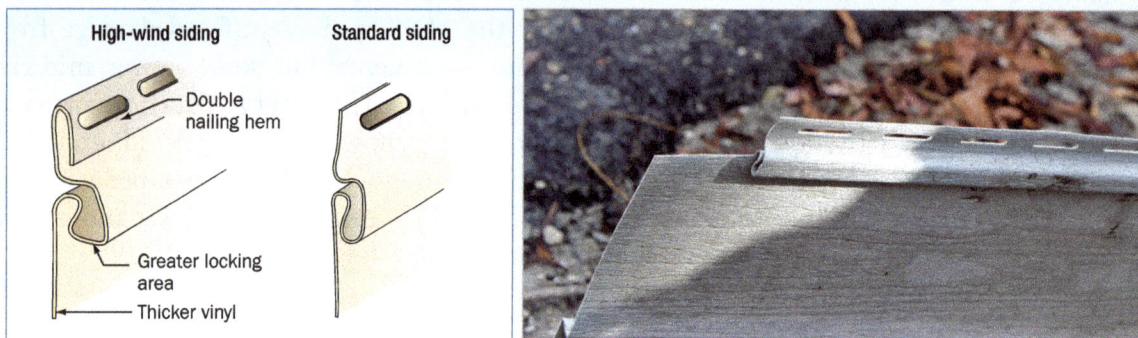

cases, vinyl soffit failure also was associated with fascia cover loss as shown in Figure 3-11. The loss of the fascia cover could have resulted in more wind exposure on the edges of soffits, affecting their performance. Refer to Florida Recovery Advisory 2, *Soffit Installation in Florida (2018c) for guidance on FBC-compliant soffit installation.*

Figure 3-11: House with metal soffit loss below missing fascia cover

3.2.4 Rooftop Equipment

The MATs observed that rooftop equipment had variable performance in high winds. While some equipment was anchored properly and remained in place during the hurricanes, many units did not. Failures of several types were observed: failure of the equipment itself (including blow off of access panels), failure of support stands or curbs, failure of attachments and guy wires, and water intrusion into mechanical penthouses. Failure of the equipment itself caused not only loss of the mechanical unit itself, but water intrusion into the building from the failed equipment. Debris that damaged roof coverings often was from the building itself. Examples of rooftop equipment failures are described below.

> **ADDITIONAL GUIDANCE**
>
> USVI Recovery Advisory 2, *Attachment of Rooftop Equipment in High Wind Regions* (FEMA 2018b), provides guidance for attaching new and existing rooftop equipment, preparations prior to hurricane landfall, and post-event assessment.

The Puerto Rico Department of Justice rooftop equipment suffered considerable damage, allowing water to enter the building. Lightning protection systems, rooftop HVAC units, and rooftop cooling towers were damaged by winds and debris in the hurricanes. Rooftop HVAC units mounted on pads were dislodged and blown across the roof, while a rooftop fan was lost entirely. A door in a rooftop cooling tower collapsed into the tower due to debris impact. Given the elevation of the cooling towers and a degree of protection from the walls surrounding the cooling tower, the impact damage was surprising and revealed unexpected vulnerabilities.

At hospitals and schools in the USVI, rooftop equipment failures led to significant water intrusion into the facilities. Wind-borne rooftop equipment debris was a primary cause of roof membrane punctures. Punctures and tears to roof membranes intensified water intrusion issues. At a 169-bed acute care facility in St. Thomas, wind forces and possible debris impacts resulted in failure of the end air intake unit, resulting in water intrusion into the building. The Cyril E. King Airport Terminal Building has a single-ply membrane at the low-slope roof and metal standing seam panels at the higher-sloped roof. Several of the metal roof and wall panels blew off during Hurricane Irma and the single-ply membrane was punctured/torn in several areas.

In Texas, common rooftop equipment failures included condenser and HVAC unit blow-off due to lack of or inadequate attachment to curbs, blow-off of HVAC unit access panels, blow-off of HVAC sheet metal unit enclosures (cabinets), blow-off of condensate drain lines, and blow-off of lightning protection systems. At the Regional Medical Center in Aransas Pass, there was extensive damage to rooftop equipment. In some places, the equipment had been inadequately attached while in others it had not been attached at all. For example, the MAT observed a rooftop condenser attached to a wood pallet that was simply resting on the roof surface.

3.2.5 Solar Heating and Photovoltaic Systems

This section covers solar heating and photovoltaic systems, including ground-mounted photovoltaic arrays and rooftop solar equipment.

3.2.5.1 Ground-Mounted Photovoltaic Arrays

The Texas, USVI, and Puerto Rico MATs observed many ground-mounted PV arrays (also known as solar arrays), each with varying degrees of damage. The MATs observed that open cross-section framing and undersized structural members and connectors were most vulnerable to damage. PV panels typically were damaged by wind-borne debris and displacement. The MATs also noted that heavily damaged PV arrays could not be tested and repaired quickly, hindering the full return of electrical utility service. See Table 4-16 in the next chapter for specific conclusions and recommendations for ground-mounted PV arrays based on the 2017 hurricane season MAT observations.

> **DESIGN GUIDANCE FOR GROUND-MOUNTED SOLAR ARRAYS**
>
> ASCE 7-16 does not provide criteria for determining wind loads on ground-mounted PV arrays. However, some guidance is provided in SEAOC PV2-17.
>
> FM Global Loss Prevention Data Sheet 7-106 provides guidelines and recommendations for the design, installation, and maintenance of ground-mounted PV arrays.

Texas

The Texas MAT observed one ground-mounted PV array after Hurricane Harvey. The panels were attached with T-bolted compression panel clips to extruded aluminum rails. Fifteen of the 64 panels were blown away, and one was damaged by wind-borne debris.

USVI

Solar power in the USVI is a rapidly growing industry, providing both distributed and utility-scale electricity for all three islands. The MAT observed a variety of solar panel arrays to determine relative performance, develop recommendations for future action, and encourage resilient rebuilding efforts. The following arrays were visited by the USVI MAT:

- The U.S. Federal Courthouse Solar Array was built and managed by the General Services Administration and was opened just before the 2017 hurricane season. Almost the entire solar array was damaged during the hurricanes.
  - The MAT observed that the cantilever design and open-section supports may have contributed to significant fluttering and vibration of the panels due to wind uplift. This exerted cyclical loading on the clips and frame, leading to failure of bolted connections.
  - The MAT observed numerous clip and fastener failures, which allowed the support arms and panels to break loose and turn into wind-borne debris that threatened the rest of the array. After the support arms were loose and twisted, individual panels were cracked and displaced.
  - At the time of the MAT observations, the array was not operational, hindering the full return of electrical service capacity.

- The Estate Spanish Town Solar Array sustained minor damage, with most frames and panels remaining completely intact. At the time of the MAT observation, the site appeared mostly undamaged, but was not operating due to limited repairs and tests needed to bring it back into service. This lack of service shows that even for minor damage to utility-scale solar arrays, disruptions to production still can last several months following a storm.

- The Estate Donoe Solar Array sustained significant damage with roughly 50 percent of panels being damaged or blown from the frames.
  - Topography appeared to play a role in protecting large portions of the array from experiencing maximum winds. However, the more exposed portions of the array were heavily damaged.
  - The combination of closed and open sections that made up the supporting structure experienced varied performance. The lower portion of the frame assemblies (columns and square tubular beams) generally performed well; however, the Z-purlins and the light-gauge metal frames supporting the solar panels experienced the most damage.
  - The array was not operational during the MAT visit.

- Two small ground-mounted arrays were observed on St. Thomas. Limited access precluded making detailed observations. However, it appeared that the damage was primarily caused by wind-borne debris.

Puerto Rico

The Puerto Rico MAT observed large ground-mounted solar arrays in Humacao, Isabela, and San Juan. Because of the differences in wind speeds and local terrain features, few direct comparisons of performance were made among these three sites.

- In Humacao, a large ground-mounted solar array belonging to Reden Solar (formerly Fonroche) experienced major damage from hurricane-wind forces and wind-borne debris. In addition to clip failure, the lateral rails and lateral rail angle connections exhibited deformation due to debris impacts or wind pressures, which lifted panels out of position. The panels then became wind-borne debris that impacted other ground-mounted arrays in a successive failure.

- In Isabela, Oriana Solar Array experienced lower wind speeds and appeared to have a more robust structural support system than the Reden array in Humacao. Overall, this array demonstrated far less damage than the Reden site, with damage or removal of approximately 10 percent of the solar panels. The Oriana Solar Array included additional structural bracing to resist wind loads.

- The Puerto Rico Convention Center Solar Array in San Juan has approximately 17,000 solar panels located over parking spaces, which offer both shade and energy production. The steel ground-mount structure and solar panels exhibited good performance and resilience during Hurricane Maria and appeared to have lost fewer than 5 percent of the solar panels to debris impact and wind uplift.

3.2.5.2 Rooftop Solar Equipment

The Texas, USVI, and Puerto Rico MATs observed rooftop solar equipment—including solar water heaters and PV power systems, as well as other rooftop systems—after Hurricanes Harvey, Irma, and Maria. See Table 4-17 in Chapter 4 for conclusions and recommendations specific to rooftop solar equipment and other systems based on the 2017 hurricane season MAT observations.

Texas

In Texas, two rooftop-mounted solar arrays were observed. In one, an entire row of panels was blown off. The panels were attached with T-bolted compression panel clips to extruded aluminum rails, which were attached with clip angles to the structure. The panels, bolts, clips, and rails were similar to a large number of arrays that were observed in the USVI. In the other rooftop solar array observed, the panels were due to be reinstalled on a newly reroofed home. During Hurricane Harvey, asphalt shingles and roof sheathing from this home were blown away, illustrating the importance of assessing the roof assembly and mitigating significant vulnerabilities before installing solar panels.

USVI

The USVI MAT noticed many rooftop PV systems on all three islands. Most of the arrays were on residences, but arrays also occurred on non-residential buildings. Some had only two panels, while others had more than 100 panels. Solar panels that are operational after a hurricane can be extremely beneficial if they can provide power to the building even if the municipal power is not operational.

The USVI MAT observed varying degrees of damage to rooftop PV systems. Several different factors can influence wind performance of PV systems, including angle of wind attack (arrays may be sensitive to certain wind directions), shielding by other buildings or topography, building height, exposure, abrupt changes in topography, wind resistance provided by the PV panels and support system, variability in installation workmanship, and degradation of resistance due to aging.

USVI RA-5 provides design and construction mitigation guidance and an overview of codes, standards, and guidelines that pertain to attachment of PV arrays.

Puerto Rico

The MAT observed rooftop solar equipment, including solar water heaters and PV power systems. The 2011 Puerto Rico Building Code forced the use of solar water heaters by requiring that only solar water heaters be used for new one- and two-family homes and townhouses, with no exemptions (Energy.gov 2018a). Overall, the observed performance of solar water heaters was excellent. This may be partly because panels on many water heater systems are attached to a more robust frame that also supports the heavy water tank. The weight of the collector also is likely greater than that of a PV array of similar area, increasing resistance to wind forces. Also, most of these systems are installed in concrete homes.

The implementation of PV power systems in residential and commercial applications has become feasible since the Government of Puerto Rico enacted net metering legislation in August 2007 (Energy.gov 2018b). In contrast to the consistently good performance of solar water heaters, the performance of PV power systems varied depending on the type of anchoring system and the type of clamping system connecting the PV panels to the aluminum frame. Most of the wind failures and damage associated with PV systems were associated with the failure of the PV panel, failure of the panel connections to the framing system, and, in some cases, lack of proper anchoring to the roof.

3.3   Implications of Poor Building Performance

Poor building performance represents a cost to the community that is more than just the cost to repair the building. Depending on the function of the building, poor performance can mean that essential services, such as healthcare, fire service, or education, are interrupted or that survivors do not have a place to live. The critical facility assessments of the MATs included an assessment of continuity of operations. Before, during, and especially after a disaster, critical facilities are only as valuable as the functions they can provide. For example, a hospital that loses all utility and backup power typically cannot provide complete medical services. Similarly, a fire station that cannot adequately protect equipment not only threatens the engines and supplies but residents throughout the area with reduced fire and rescue capacity.

3.3.1   Residential Buildings

Residential building damage varied across the four states and territories visited by the MATs. Damage to residential buildings, especially when coupled with short- or long-term loss of utility services, may mean that survivors are unable to live in their homes. This requires congregate and non-congregate sheltering options and sometimes relocation out of the affected area entirely.

The Texas MAT studied the effects of NFIP participation and how different flood-resistant building characteristics related to insurance claim payments in Harris County. See Section 3.1.5.2 of FEMA P-2022, *Mitigation Assessment Team Report: Hurricane Harvey in Texas*, for details (FEMA 2019).

3.3.2   Non-Residential Buildings

Many of the non-residential buildings observed by the MATs served governmental functions. Damage to these facilities often was caused by the entry of wind-driven rain, damaging the interior of the building and, in many cases, requiring closure.

Impacts to operations for most of the non-residential buildings observed were caused primarily by water intrusion with or without loss of power. Loss of power exacerbated damage due to water intrusion by preventing clean-up and mitigation using electric-powered equipment, including air conditioners, fans, and dehumidifiers. The lack of air movement, lack of moisture and humidity control, and growth of mold and mildew delayed recovery.

For example, the Puerto Rico MAT assessed several mid-rise buildings (having from 5 to approximately 10 floors), all of which had governmental functions. Mid-rise buildings typically had reinforced concrete cores and did not suffer structural damage from wind. The facilities visited by the Puerto Rico MAT were all sited well and remained above or outside areas of flooding. However, the MAT observed considerable damage to and loss from these buildings due to breaches and failures that admitted wind and wind-driven rain.

3.3.3   Critical Facilities

Critical facilities are the first line of response to severe weather events and provide necessary public services that are required before, during, and immediately after a hurricane. First responders use these facilities to manage emergency operations, provide healthcare, and ensure the active safety and security of residents. Even minor damage to buildings such as hospitals, fire stations, police stations, schools, and communications infrastructure hubs can render them inoperable and inhibit the provision of services. Many critical facilities impacted by the storms suffered significant damage. Much of the damage was caused by wind-driven rain infiltrating the facilities through penetrations in the roof or glazing breakage, damaging the interior space. This damage impacted the ability of these facilities to provide critical services following the hurricanes.

3.3.3.1 Hospitals

All three of the primary hospitals / healthcare facilities in the USVI experienced damage and service losses from the impacts of Hurricanes Irma and Maria.

Because Hurricane Maria affected nearly all of Puerto Rico, individual hospitals did not have the option to relocate their patients to other facilities until the storm passed. High winds and wind-driven rain damaged hospital facilities, while prolonged power outages impeded services and threatened stores of medicines. Many hospitals suffered extensive physical damage that resulted in complete loss of function. Others worked to continue life-saving care in the face of frequent power outages, limited supplies, and limited usable space. Most hospitals in Puerto Rico were not outfitted with emergency and backup generators designed to provide power for full facility operation for a number of months. As time progressed, hospitals lost main, standby, and backup power as equipment became stressed beyond its duty cycle. Fuel demand also became a limiting factor, with full demand consumption rates requiring fuel deliveries as often as every four days. Without power, many critical functions of the hospitals were only intermittently available.

The Texas MAT visited a regional medical center in Aransas Pass to observe wind-related damage. This older facility had an aggregate surfaced built-up roof over a steel deck and joists. A large portion of the roof membrane over the emergency room area blew off. In one area, the blow-off appeared to be initiated by the lifting of the top nailer flashing to which the gutter was attached. In other areas, gutter uplift initiated the blow-off. There was extensive damage to rooftop equipment and wind-borne equipment may have punctured the roof membrane in some locations. Evacuation of the hospital began the day before the hurricane made landfall and was completed the next afternoon and the facility was closed. Repairing the facility was considered, but it was determined that it was more cost-effective to build a new facility.

> ### TEXAS MEDICAL CENTER
>
> After Hurricane Harvey, the Texas MAT visited six of the Texas Medical Center (TMC) member institutions where dry floodproofing measures were implemented. Most of the buildings visited by the MAT are located in Shaded Zone X (outside of the SFHA) and are exempt from the flood provisions of model codes and standards such as the IBC and ASCE 24. Although not required, TMC installed numerous flood-resistant features and developed an extensive emergency operations plan for hurricanes. In general, the majority of facilities at TMC suffered only a minimal amount of floodwater intrusion and damage during Hurricane Harvey. This was a result of the facilities owners' proactive approaches to flood hazard mitigation over the past 15 to 20 years, rigorous emergency preparedness policies and procedures, and the significant amount of channel capacity improvements to the Harris Gully box culvert and Brays Bayou that adjoin the TMC campus.

3.3.3.2 Police, Fire, and Emergency Medical Services

Fire stations observed in the USVI sustained varying levels of damage from minor to complete loss of function. Common problems included power loss, flooding, bay door failure, and glazing and roof covering damage. In several facilities, damage to the building envelope led to water intrusion and interior damage.

In the USVI, numerous communication towers, radio repeaters, and local landlines were damaged during both Hurricanes Irma and Maria, making it difficult to communicate with fire department personnel in other locations.

The Puerto Rico MAT assessed several fire and police stations. The facilities observed were built with reinforced concrete and did not suffer any structural damage. Impacts to operations typically were due to flooding of records and issues with generators. Generators at several of the facilities failed when flooded, and one generator, though elevated, suffered mechanical failures unrelated to flooding and was sited improperly, causing fumes to enter enclosed portions of the facility.

3.3.3.3 Schools

Many schools suffered significant damage to the interior spaces and contents due to failures in the building envelope and structural elements. For those not being used as shelters, this resulted in a loss of function.

In the USVI, damage to schools caused by Hurricanes Irma and Maria was extensive. Two months after the hurricanes, two thirds of the schools on St. Croix still were not open. The extended period of high humidity and water inundation due to failures of the building envelope and structure caused direct damage and allowed microbial damage to the schools. Many of the older buildings that had little superstructure damage have asbestos in the floor tiles and mastic adhesives, making them unsuitable for immediate occupancy before decontamination.

On September 21, the day after Hurricane Maria made landfall, all school buildings in Puerto Rico were closed except those being used as shelters. Impacts to school facilities were widespread and it was not until early December that 1,075, or more than 90 percent, of the schools reopened. During that time, many schools opened with water and basic school services, but a number of buildings were reopened without power, or without full power, limiting some of the activities at the schools. The Puerto Rico Department of Education reported that 38 schools have been identified as unable to be reopened because of extensive building damage that they would not repair.

All of the schools visited by the Texas MAT experienced roof system damage and interior damage due to roof leakage. Most or all of the roof damage was caused by punctures or tears to roof membranes, displaced rooftop equipment, or damaged or displaced flashing. Breaches in the rooftop systems allowed rainwater to enter, causing widespread interior water damage.

3.3.3.4 Community Safe Rooms and Storm Shelters

Safe rooms and storm shelters are structures designed and constructed to provide near-absolute protection during extreme-wind events, providing protection against both wind pressures and wind-borne debris impacts. Though similar, there are important differences between safe rooms and storm shelters. While both must meet all requirements of ICC 500, *ICC/NSSA Standard for the Design and Construction of Storm Shelters* (ICC 2008), safe rooms also meet the recommended criteria for safe rooms described in FEMA P-361, *Safe Rooms for Tornadoes and Hurricanes: Guidance for Community and Residential Safe Rooms* (FEMA 2015a); these criteria are slightly more conservative than those presented in ICC 500 for storm shelters.

Few, if any, public safe rooms or storm shelters have been constructed in the USVI and Puerto Rico. The existing buildings being used as hurricane evacuation shelters, best available refuge areas, or post-event shelters were likely not designed to provide life-safety protection from hurricanes. The buildings serving as emergency shelters in Puerto Rico and the USVI had not been evaluated by design professionals for flood, wind, and seismic vulnerabilities, and none were designed in accordance with FEMA P-361 or ICC 500 for protection for residents during hurricanes.

In the USVI and Puerto Rico, many of the school buildings identified as emergency shelters experienced significant damage, including damage to structural elements as well as loss of power and communications.

3.3.3.5 Residential Safe Rooms

The Puerto Rico MAT visited five residential safe rooms on Culebra that were designed and constructed to meet FEMA P-361 criteria using Hazard Mitigation Grant Program (HMGP) funding after Hurricane Georges. The MAT observed no damage to any of the residential safe rooms on Culebra following Hurricanes Irma and Maria. However, some had been extensively modified to allow for air ventilation, for sleeping and cooking—modifications that increased the vulnerabilities of the buildings. Although no damage was observed, these buildings no longer comply with FEMA P-361 and cannot be relied on to perform the intended purpose of near-absolute protection of their occupants.

COMPENDIUM REPORT
2017
HURRICANE SEASON

4 Conclusions and Recommendations

Conclusions and recommendations from the MAT reports are organized by topic in the following subsections: General Conclusions and Recommendations; Building Codes, Standards, and Regulations; Flood-Related Building Performance; Wind-Related Building Performance; and FEMA Technical Publications and Guidance. For more information about the conclusions and recommendations, refer to the individual MAT Reports:

- FEMA P-2020, *Mitigation Assessment Team Report: Hurricanes Irma and Maria in Puerto Rico* (FEMA 2018a)

- FEMA P-2021, *Mitigation Assessment Team Report: Hurricanes Irma and Maria in the U.S. Virgin Islands* (FEMA 2018b)

- FEMA P-2022, *Mitigation Assessment Team Report: Hurricane Harvey in Texas* (FEMA 2019)

- FEMA P-2023, *Mitigation Assessment Team Report: Hurricane Irma in Florida* (FEMA 2018c)

4.1 General Conclusions and Recommendations

The Texas, Puerto Rico, and USVI MATs all observed that facility and building owners have limited awareness of their hazard risks and vulnerabilities. The quality of planning and preparedness at the non-residential buildings visited by the MATs—particularly some schools, nursing homes, and medical centers along the coast—varied greatly. Many building managers and owners may not have been aware of the higher risks to their buildings from such severe hurricane events. Table 4-1 presents the general MAT conclusions and recommendations related to awareness of hurricane hazard risks and vulnerabilities.

Table 4-1: General Conclusions and Recommendations

Conclusions	Recommendations
PR-2, USVI-3, TX-2. Many building owners had limited awareness of hurricane hazard risks and vulnerabilities.	**PR-2, USVI-3, TX-2.** Facility and building owners should perform vulnerability assessments for all relevant hazards prior to a natural hazard event.
PR-9. Few homeowners in Puerto Rico have flood insurance and, of those that do, the majority have private flood insurance.	• **PR-9a.** FEMA should work with the Insurance Institute for Business & Home Safety (IBHS) to review private flood insurance policies for equivalency and effectiveness. • **PR-9b.** FEMA, in conjunction with IBHS, should develop materials, outreach, and partnerships to educate homeowners on flood insurance options (both private and NFIP) and its importance.

4.2 Building Codes, Standards, and Regulations

This section includes MAT conclusions and recommendations related to building codes, standards, and regulations. The tables in this section are organized by topic in the following subsections: Adoption of Codes and Regulations, Enforcement, Staffing and Training, and New Requirements or Amendments. See Chapter 2 for MAT observations about building codes, standards, and regulations relating to the 2017 hurricane season.

4.2.1 Adoption of Codes and Regulations

To better resist the impacts of hurricanes, floods, and seismic events, the latest edition of the building code and other hazard-resistant regulations should be considered for adoption. During the assessment process, the MATs reviewed the codes and regulations in effect in the states and territories they observed. Table 4-2 presents the MAT conclusions and recommendations related to the adoption of the latest model building codes and referenced standards. Note that two of the Puerto Rico MAT recommendations, PR-3a and PR-3b, resulted in the adoption of updated codes.

Table 4-2: Adoption of Codes and Regulations

Conclusions	Recommendations
PR-3, USVI-4. The PR and USVI building codes are not consistent with the latest model building codes and lack process for update and amendment.	• **PR-3a, USVI-1a, USVI-4a.** Adopt or update codes to be consistent with latest hazard-resistant building codes and standards. • **PR-3b, USVI-4a.** Specify a recurring code update cycle. • **USVI-4b.** Provide published process for stakeholders to suggest amendments to the building code.
PR-11, USVI-13, TX-4. Floodplain management ordinances are out of date or conflict with model building code requirements and updates.	**PR-11, USVI-13, TX4a-e.** Update local floodplain management ordinances, regulations, and guidance to be consistent with model building codes (e.g., IBC and IRC).
USVI-5. The referenced building code is not clearly presented or defined (named code, edition, and year) with the local amendments.	**USVI-5.** DPNR should use multiple means of media (print, website, etc.) to identify the current edition of the I-Codes that is being referenced as the USVI Building Code (including appendices) and list all local amendments.
TX-3. The TDI Texas Windstorm Inspection Program requirements are based on compliance with the 2006 IBC and IRC, which are outdated.	• **TX-3a.** TDI should adopt the 2018 IBC and IRC as the model codes for its Windstorm Inspection Program. • **TX-3b.** TDI should consider developing a more stringent high-wind retrofit program.

4.2.2 Enforcement

When hazard-resistant codes and regulations are adopted, they also must be enforced properly to be effective in reducing vulnerability to hazard events. All four of the MATs observed instances where codes and regulations were not being enforced properly, which led to vulnerabilities and resulted in damage during the 2017 hurricane season. Table 4-3 presents the MAT conclusions and recommendations related to the enforcement of hazard-resistant codes and regulations.

Table 4-3: Enforcement

Conclusions	Recommendations
FL-1, TX-1. Building codes and floodplain management requirements were inconsistently enforced.	• **FL-1a, TX-1b.** The Florida Division of Emergency Management (FDEM) and the Texas Water Development Board should develop / modify training on the flood provisions in the model building codes and / or local floodplain management ordinances. • **FL-1b.** Building Officials Association of Florida, Florida Home Builders Association, and other stakeholders should consider developing additional training placing emphasis on building envelope components. • **TX-1a.** Continue providing training to Windstorm Inspection Program inspectors and building code enforcement staff, placing emphasis on changes reflected in the latest adopted edition of the building code.
PR-10. Administrative Order 2017-07 (OGPe) exempted certain recovery efforts and essential activities from ordinary construction permits.	• **PR-10a.** Develop a process for documentation of short-term, post-disaster repairs. • **PR-10b.** Develop process for retroactive permit review of rebuilding and repairs.
PR-17. Many non-code-compliant homes exist throughout Puerto Rico.	**PR-17.** Develop processes for bringing noncompliant buildings into compliance.
USVI-11. USVI lacks key material resources to help DPNR enforce codes.	• **USVI-11a.** Maintain a list of select tested and approved hazard-resistant materials for key systems. • **USVI-11b.** Work with local construction material suppliers to ensure that tested and approved materials are available in store for homeowners and building owners for rebuilding.
TX-11, FL-3. States and communities did not receive (or did not receive in a timely manner) data on buildings that appeared to have incurred Substantial Damage.	**TX-11, FL-3.** FEMA should develop an effective and timely means to deliver the Adjuster Preliminary Damage Assessment data.
TX-9. Non-flood-damage-resistant materials were used below the Base Flood Elevation (BFE) in elevated buildings and had to be replaced.	**TX-9.** Local floodplain administrators must enforce, and design professionals and builders must comply with, the requirement to use flood-damage-resistant materials below an elevated building's Design Flood Elevation (DFE).
PR-27. It is common practice and permissible under the building code to use prescriptive home designs in residential construction.	**PR-27.** OGPe, with support from stakeholders, should develop prescriptive design plans and make them available to support affordable, code-compliant construction of homes and residential buildings.

4.2.3 Staffing and Training

To enforce building codes and regulations, adequately trained staff is necessary to conduct plan reviews, responsibly issue permits, and perform inspection to ensure compliance. Table 4-4 presents the MAT conclusions and recommendations to support building code officials and others that perform compliance and enforcement activities.

Table 4-4: Staffing and Training

Conclusions	Recommendations
PR-6, USVI-8, FL-2. Building officials lack adequate staffing, which limits their ability to perform compliance and enforcement activities and to conduct post-disaster inspections.	• **PR-6, USVI-8, FL-2.** Conduct evaluations of staffing requirements and gaps for routine compliance and enforcement activities and post-disaster code inspection needs. Include State Mutual Aid Agreement (SMAA) resources in evaluation. • **PR-6c.** Municipalities should consider participating in the Insurance Service Office's (ISO) Building Codes Effectiveness Grading Schedule (BCEGS).
PR-7, USVI-9. Training was insufficient for code enforcement staff and in-house technical experts.	**PR-7, USVI-9.** Provide training to building code enforcement staff on the latest edition of the referenced code that has been adopted.
PR-8. Licensure and training of design professionals and contractors positively affected quality.	• **PR-8a.** Establish a licensure program for contractors in Puerto Rico. • **PR-8b.** Train design professionals and contractors on the latest hazard-resistant design and construction techniques and best practices. • **PR-8c.** Establish a public database of actively licensed and registered design professionals and contractors.
PR-12. Not every community has a Certified Floodplain Manager (CFM).	**PR-12.** All NFIP communities and autonomous municipalities that actively issue construction permits should have a Certified Floodplain Manager or equivalent on staff.
PR-13. Only a single community in Puerto Rico, Ponce, participates in the CRS.	• **PR-13a.** FEMA Region II should conduct outreach to Puerto Rico on the benefits of participating in the CRS. • **PR-13b.** The PRPB should encourage participation in the CRS for communities that would benefit.
FL-5. FDEM documented the successful completion of its multi-year CRS initiative.	**FL-5.** FDEM should expand its technical assistance for CRS communities.

4.2.4 New Requirements or Amendments

All four of the MATs identified potential requirements or amendments that could strengthen the hazard resistance of structures and enhance community disaster resilience. Five of the Puerto Rico MAT recommendations, PR-3a, PR-3b, PR-4, PR-21, and PR-35a, resulted in the adoption of six amendments to the PRBC. Two of the Florida MAT recommendations, FL-10b and FL-11b, are currently being considered during the FBC update process. Table 4-5 presents the MAT conclusions and recommendations for new requirements or amendments to support hazard-resistant design and construction and enhance community resilience.

Table 4-5: New Requirements or Amendments

Conclusions	Recommendations
PR-4. Corrosion of fasteners and connectors contributed to building failures throughout Puerto Rico.	**PR-4.** Amend PRBC to require corrosion-resistant materials for fasteners and connectors.
PR-5, USVI-12. Staged or phased construction remains exposed to the elements, degrading exposed structural elements over time.	• **PR-5a, USVI-12b.** Protect material during staged or phased construction. • **PR-5b, USVI-12a.** Limit extended open permit periods for staged or phased construction.
PR-14. FIRMs for Puerto Rico do not delineate Coastal A Zones.	• **PR-14.** Ensure new ABFE maps and FIRMs depict the Limit of Moderate Wave Action on all appropriate map products.
USVI-2. Numerous temporary facilities are vulnerable to wind hazards and have been installed for longer than their intended purpose.	**USVI-2.** The permitted use of temporary buildings should be limited to 180 days, as set forth in the IBC.
USVI-6. Requirements for signing and sealing construction documents are too permissive in the USVI Building Code.	**USVI-6.** Amend the USVI Building Code and restrict the signing and sealing of construction documents to registered design professionals.
USVI-7. Building damage / repair triggers in the USVI Building Code based solely on financial replacement costs for buildings / systems can be simplified.	**USVI-7.** DPNR should amend the current code for percent damage repair triggers.
PR-21, USVI-10. OGPe and DPNR do not provide a list of specific notes and design criteria for design professionals to include on construction drawings.	**PR-21, USVI-10.** OGPe and DPNR should consider requiring construction documents to list critical design parameters, including hazard-resistant design criteria, and require load path connections be shown.

Conclusions	Recommendations
PR-35, USVI-31. The MAT observed no shelters designed in accordance with FEMA P-361 or ICC 500 for protection for residents during hurricanes.	**PR-35a, USVI-31a.** Require specific educational and first responder facilities to provide a storm shelter.
TX-10. Damage to buildings not designed and constructed to current building code requirements was noticeably greater than damage to code- and NFIP-compliant buildings.	• **TX-10a.** When and where possible, FEMA should update the NFIP standards to be at least equivalent to the consensus-based codes. • **TX-10b.** FEMA and communities should re-evaluate the criteria for Substantial Improvement / Substantial Damage.
FL-6. Florida's installation requirements for MHUs do not reference the current edition of FEMA 85.	**FL-6.** The Florida Department of Highway Safety and Motor Vehicles should reference the most recent edition of FEMA P-85.
FL 10. The MAT observed evidence of inadequate resistance to wind pressures and improper installation of soffits on residential buildings.	**FL-10b.** The FBC should require soffit inspections. Soffit inspections will help to ensure compliant products are used and the soffit is securely attached.
FL 11. The MAT observed evidence of inadequate resistance to wind pressures for certain wall coverings of residential buildings.	**FL-11b.** The FBC should require wall cladding inspections.

4.3 Flood-Related Building Performance

This section includes MAT conclusions and recommendations about flood-related building performance during the 2017 hurricane season. The tables in this section are organized by topic in the following subsections: General Conclusions and Recommendations; Slope Stability, Erosion and Scour; and Dry Floodproofing. The MATs observed that flood-related building damage was primarily attributable to non-elevated or low-elevation buildings, siting issues, dry floodproofing failures, the use of non-flood-damage-resistant materials below the BFE, and widespread flooding outside the SFHA. See Section 3.1 for details about MAT observations of flood-related building performance during the 2017 hurricane season.

4.3.1 General Conclusions and Recommendations

The Texas, Puerto Rico, and USVI MATs made important observations, conclusions, and recommendations about flood insurance, flood-risk research and education, vulnerability assessments, implementation of flood-risk reduction measures, and best practices that can reduce vulnerability to flood risk. Table 4-6 presents the general MAT conclusions and recommendations for flood-related building performance during the 2017 hurricane season.

Table 4-6: General Conclusions and Recommendations for Flood Hazards

Conclusions	Recommendations
PR-16. Schools have been consolidated into facilities that remain vulnerable to flood hazards.	**PR-16.** The PRDE should consider performing a vulnerability assessment of existing buildings in planning consolidation of schools.
TX-12. The MAT observed widespread flood damage both within and outside the regulatory floodplain.	• **TX-12a.** FEMA should make NFIP policy information, especially data related to historical claims, available to help supplement flood hazard data on the FIRM. • **TX-12b.** Owners of buildings located near but outside the SFHA should consider implementing flood-risk reduction measures.
PR-46. The use of flood-damage-resistant materials minimized damage and facilitated recovery.	**PR-46.** Building owners should use flood-damage-resistant materials in existing concrete and CMU buildings.
PR-20, USVI-16. Excessive water intrusion through existing exterior doors was observed.	**PR-20, USVI-16.** Mitigate exterior doors with improved water intrusion resistance.
PR-23. Building utilities are at risk of flood damage.	**PR-23.** Building owners should elevate critical systems whenever possible.
PR-28, USVI-23, TX-5. Many non-elevated or low-elevation buildings with floors at or near adjacent grade sustained flood damage.	• **PR-28, USVI-23, TX-5a.** Communities and building owners should consider elevating new and Substantially Improved or Substantially Damaged buildings at least above grade, and above the NFIP elevation requirements (if they apply) to protect the buildings from flooding. • **TX-5b.** Communities should incorporate the best-available flood hazard data wherever possible. • **TX-5c.** Communities should consider future conditions in zoning, building code, and floodplain management requirements.
TX-13. Contractors and designers have insufficient guidance on elevated slab projects.	**TX-13.** Continue ongoing research on the performance of elevated slab foundations and develop related outreach material.

4.3.2 Slope Stability, Erosion, and Scour

Both the Puerto Rico and Florida MATs observed buildings that were damaged because they were sited in areas vulnerable to slope stability hazards, erosion, and scour. See Section 3.1.2.2 for details about MAT observations on the impacts of erosion and scour on building performance during the 2017 hurricane season. Table 4-7 presents the MAT conclusions and recommendations related to slope stability, erosion, and scour.

Table 4-7: Slope Stability, Erosion, and Scour

Conclusions	Recommendations
PR-37. Many buildings were observed in highly vulnerable locations.	• **PR-37a.** Puerto Rico and local municipalities should consider acquisition of highly vulnerable buildings. • **PR-37b.** FEMA and the USGS should consider development of enhanced guidance for addressing slope stability and erosion vulnerabilities for new and existing construction. • **PR-37c.** OGPe should require documentation of geotechnical review for areas with slope stability concerns. • **PR-37d.** OGPe should require erosion vulnerability assessment for new construction in known erosion hazard areas.
FL-4. The MAT observed damaged buildings that illustrate the problems associated with siting buildings on erodible shorelines.	• **FL-4a.** Permitting agencies should evaluate permitting criteria and performance requirements for new or replacement bulkheads. • **FL-4b.** FEMA should review and update their event-based erosion methodology.

4.3.3 Dry Floodproofing

Both the Texas and Florida MATs were tasked with evaluating how dry floodproofing systems had performed during Hurricanes Harvey and Irma. See Section 3.1.3 for details about MAT observations of non-residential buildings with dry floodproofing during the 2017 hurricane season. Table 4-8 presents the MAT conclusions and recommendations related to dry floodproofing performance.

Table 4-8: Dry Floodproofing

Conclusions	Recommendations
TX-6, FL-7. Dry floodproofing measures often failed under less than design flood conditions.	• **TX-6a-b, FL-7.** Local floodplain administrators, design professionals, and building owners should follow FEMA's Texas Recovery Advisory 1 and Florida Recovery Advisory 1. • **TX-6b.** Local floodplain administrators, design professionals, and building owners should ensure sump pumps, with a floor drain system to collect seepage, are included as part of all dry floodproofing systems.
TX-7. Dry floodproofed buildings that were considered substantially impermeable sustained damage that resulted in significant loss of function.	**TX-7.** Flood-damage-resistant materials should be used below the dry floodproofed elevation inside dry floodproofed buildings when possible.
TX-8, FL-8. Dry floodproofed buildings where building managers had instilled a culture of preparedness sustained less damage than other dry floodproofed buildings.	**TX-8a, FL-8a.** Facility managers should develop an emergency operations plan for severe weather. **TX-8b, FL-8b.** Facility managers should routinely re-evaluate dry floodproofing designs and plans as required by codes and standards. **TX-8c, FL-8c.** Facility managers should take reasonable measures to instill a culture of preparedness.

4.4 Wind-Related Building Performance

This section includes MAT conclusions and recommendations about wind-related building performance during the 2017 hurricane season. The tables in this section are organized by topic in the following subsections: General Conclusions and Recommendations, Topographic Effects on Wind Speeds, Structural Systems / Main Wind Force Resisting Systems, Manufactured Housing, Openings, Roof Coverings, Exterior Wall Coverings, Soffits, Ground-Mounted Photovoltaic Systems, Rooftop Systems and Solar Equipment, and Shelters.

The MATs observed wind-induced failures of building envelope components, connections, and systems that allowed wind-driven rain to enter the building's interior, resulting in costly damage. Damage to roof coverings, rooftop equipment, soffits, exterior wall coverings, glazed openings, and sectional garage doors was observed to be widespread. See Section 3.2 for details about MAT observations of wind-related building performance during the 2017 hurricane season.

4.4.1 General Conclusions and Recommendations

The Puerto Rico and USVI MATs had key observations, conclusions, and recommendations about vulnerabilities in existing buildings and deficiencies in structural load paths. The USVI MAT also noted that the HPRP roof replacement program worked well and recommends the development of a new retrofit program to address roofing, structural, and building envelope issues in a comprehensive approach to wind mitigation. Table 4-9 presents the general MAT conclusions and recommendations for wind-related building performance during the 2017 hurricane season.

Table 4-9: General Conclusions and Recommendations for Wind Hazards

Conclusions	Recommendations
PR-25, USVI-18. Key wind and seismic vulnerabilities remain in many undamaged homes.	**PR-25, USVI-18.** Homeowners should consider evaluating and retrofitting existing homes for wind and seismic vulnerabilities.
PR-1, USVI-1. Many damaged buildings lacked a continuous load path.	• **PR-1a.** Develop and publish prescriptive design guidance and load path details for designers and contractors. • **PR-1b.** Require construction documents to list critical design parameters and show load path connections. • **USVI-1b.** USVI Department of Planning and Natural Resources should continue to update the *Stronger Home Guide* as the IBC and IRC are updated.
USVI-19. HPRP roof design, when implemented correctly, performed well.	**USVI-19.** Develop and support a wind retrofit program across USVI.

4.4.2 Topographic Effects on Wind Speeds

Both the USVI and Puerto Rico MATs observed that mountainous topography increased wind speeds and led to increased wind-related damage to vulnerably sited buildings. See Section 3.2.1 for details about MAT observations regarding the topographic effects of wind speeds on building performance during the 2017 hurricane season. Table 4-10 presents the MAT conclusions and recommendations related to siting and topographic effects.

Table 4-10: Siting and Topographic Effects

Conclusions	Recommendations
PR-36. Topography increased wind speeds throughout mountainous areas of Puerto Rico. **USVI-40.** Buildings generally lacked designs that considered topographic effects, thereby increasing damage.	• **PR-36.** Develop new design guidance for wind speed-up in Puerto Rico. • **USVI-40a.** DPNR should work with the Legislature to incorporate revised basic wind speed maps into the USVI Building Code that consider topographic effects as an option to determine wind pressures on buildings. • **USVI-40b.** DPNR should consider developing guidance to assist designers when applying the microzoning wind maps. • **USVI-40c.** The revised basic wind speed maps developed for the USVI should be proposed for inclusion in the next edition.

4.4.3 Manufactured Housing

During the 2017 hurricane season, the Florida and USVI MATs observed that damage to MHUs was caused primarily by wind hazards. See Section 3.2.2.5 for details about MAT observations of manufactured housing performance during the 2017 hurricane season. Table 4-11 presents the MAT conclusions and recommendations related to manufactured housing.

Table 4-11: Manufactured Housing

Conclusions	Recommendations
USVI-21. Many MHUs experienced near-total damage from a wind event that was at or below design levels for the USVI.	**USVI-21.** Ensure MHUs are properly designed and installed for their given HUD wind zones throughout USVI.
USVI-22. MHU labeling often had been removed, making it difficult to identify units.	• **USVI-22a.** DPNR should require MHU labels or placards to be maintained on all MHUs regardless of age or the renovation of the unit. • **USVI-22b.** HUD should consider location of MHU labels or placards such that any renovation of the exterior material, sun damage, or water damage does not cover the label.
FL-13. Failure of appurtenance attachments to MHUs increased the units' vulnerability to wind and rain damage.	**FL-13.** As a best practice, manufactured housing appurtenances should be built as standalone units without structural connection to the MHU.

4.4.4 Openings

All four of the MATs observed many types of openings (glazed windows, open / louvered window assemblies, sectional garage doors, and others) that failed under wind pressures or impacts from wind-borne debris, leaving structures vulnerable to internal wind pressures, wind-driven rain, or other damage. See Section 3.2.3.1 for details about MAT observations regarding building openings during the 2017 hurricane season. Table 4-12 presents the MAT conclusions and recommendations related to the performance of openings.

Table 4-12: Openings

Conclusions	Recommendations
PR-18, USVI-14, TX-15. Windows (glazed openings) on most existing buildings are vulnerable to damage and failure from wind pressures and wind-borne debris.	• **PR-18a-c, TX-15a, USVI-14a-c.** Critical facility owners, homeowners, building owners, and property managers of commercial and large, multi-unit residential buildings should protect windows on existing buildings. • **PR-18d.** Building owners should consider developing a lifecycle management program for roof coverings, rooftop equipment restraints, and opening protection systems. • **TX-15b.** FEMA should ensure that opening protection is incorporated into eligible Public Assistance Hazard Mitigation Proposals.
PR-19, USVI-15. Water intrusion through and around existing windows (glazed openings) and metal panel jalousie systems was pervasive.	• **PR-19, USVI-15a.** Replace older glazed (glass) openings in existing buildings with new windows designed and tested to resist water intrusion and windborne debris. • **USVI-15b.** Consider using water-damage-resistant materials to address water intrusion for interior spaces that have exterior jalousie window systems.
USVI-30. Large, overhead roll-up doors failed under wind loading and debris impact at critical facilities.	• **USVI-30.** Use only large overhead doors that have been tested and certified for wind loads and debris impact associated with the design criteria for the site.
PR-29, USVI-24. Internal pressures were not addressed adequately through open / louvered window assemblies.	• **PR-29a, USVI-24.** Designers must consider and adequately address internal wind pressures. • **PR-29b.** Consider retrofitting glazed openings, windows, and doors of existing buildings for current wind design pressures and wind-borne debris protection.
TX-20. The performance of high-wind-rated sectional and rolling doors was noticeably better than those that were not designed for use in high-wind regions.	**TX-20.** Building owners in the hurricane-prone regions should have sectional and rolling doors evaluated and replace existing doors that lack adequate resistance.

Conclusions	Recommendations
TX-22. Current testing standards may need to further consider debris impact.	• **TX-22a.** FEMA should work with industry partners to evaluate whether ASTM testing requirements for debris impacts and wind pressures should be adjusted. • **TX-22b.** Industry groups and / or academia should study debris generation and strikes to protective systems during hurricanes to determine whether the wind speed triggers for the ASCE 7 wind-borne debris region are appropriate.
FL-12. The MAT observed evidence of windborne debris, but very few instances of glazed openings being breached.	• **FL-12a.** Industry groups and / or academia should study debris generation and strikes to protective systems during hurricanes to determine whether the wind speed triggers for the ASCE 7 wind-borne debris region are appropriate. • **FL-12b.** Building owners outside the wind-borne debris region should consider protecting the glazed openings on their buildings.

4.4.5 Roof Coverings

All four of the MATs observed damage to roof coverings caused by inadequate installation, leakage around displaced rooftop equipment, roof materials and rooftop equipment anchorage with inadequate resistance to wind loads, and the use of single-ply roof membranes. See Section 3.2.3.2 for details about MAT observations of roof coverings during the 2017 hurricane season. Table 4-13 presents the MAT conclusions and recommendations related to the performance of roof coverings.

Table 4-13: Roof Coverings

Conclusions	Recommendations
PR-22. Tile roofs resulted in poor performance.	**PR-22.** Evaluate existing tile roofs for proper anchorage and connectors.
PR-24, USVI-17. Lack of roof deck (sheathing) under roof panel coverings resulted in increased damage.	**PR-24, USVI-17.** Require the use of wood deck on wood-framed roofs below any roof covering.
PR-26. Roof penetrations often caused water intrusion.	**PR-26.** Avoid rooftop penetrations whenever possible.
USVI-20. Utility service mast roof penetrations through roof coverings performed poorly.	**USVI-20.** Avoid penetrating roof coverings, including porches and overhangs, with utility service masts.
PR-30, USVI-25, USVI-26. Insufficient installation and maintenance of roof coverings resulted in increased damage.	• **PR-30a, USVI-26.** Regularly assess, adequately maintain, and repair or replace roofs when needed. • **PR-30b, USVI-25b.** Avoid the use of single-ply roof membranes. • **USVI-25a.** Design and install new and replacement roof coverings for critical facilities to resist high winds in accordance with ASCE 7-16.
PR-31. Debris that damaged roof coverings often was from the building itself.	**PR-31.** Adequately anchor HVAC and other equipment to roof.
TX-17, FL-9. Inadequate resistance to wind loads caused asphalt shingle and other residential roof covering damage.	• **TX-17, FL-9b.** Contractors should use, and inspectors should enforce the use of, asphalt roof shingles rated for high-wind regions and follow special installation methods to increase wind resistance. • **FL-9a.** Industry groups should investigate the causes for the widespread asphalt shingle roof covering loss that was observed by the MAT.
TX-21. The improved wind performance of metal edge flashings and copings in new construction contributed to the reduced number of roof membrane blow-offs.	**TX-21.** Building owners with single-ply roof membranes should ensure their metal edge systems are properly installed.

4.4.6 Exterior Wall Coverings

Both the Texas and Florida MATs observed residential wall coverings that had inadequate resistance to wind pressures leading to widespread loss of these coverings. In some cases, the loss of these materials served as an initiation point for progressive damage. See Section 3.2.3.3 for details about MAT observations of exterior wall coverings during the 2017 hurricane season. Table 4-14 presents the MAT conclusions and recommendations related to exterior wall coverings.

Table 4-14: Exterior Wall Coverings

Conclusions	Recommendations
TX-16, FL-11. Residential wall coverings had inadequate resistance to wind pressures, causing widespread loss of these coverings, which, in some cases, served as an initiation point for progressive damage.	• **TX-16a.** Design professionals should specify, and contractors should use, face nails on fiber cement siding. • **TX-16b, FL-11b.** Windstorm inspectors and local building officials should enforce the use of approved materials in high-wind regions and ensure they are installed in accordance with the manufacturer's requirements. • **FL-11a.** Vinyl siding manufacturers, insurance organizations, and other stakeholders should continue investigations of the appropriate pressure equalization factor for vinyl siding. • **FL-11b.** The FBC should require wall cladding inspections.
TX-19. Brick veneer failures were common.	**TX-19.** Design professionals and contractors should improve installation of brick veneer in high-wind regions.

4.4.7 Soffits

Both the Texas and Florida MATs observed soffit failures caused by improper installation or the use of improper materials. See Section 3.2.3.4 for details about MAT observations of soffits during the 2017 hurricane season. Table 4-15 presents the MAT conclusions and recommendations related to soffits.

Table 4-15: Soffits

Conclusions	Recommendations
TX-18, FL-10. Many soffits lacked adequate wind resistance, typically because the wrong material was used for the region or it was improperly installed.	• **TX-18, FL-10a.** Designers, contractors, and inspectors should place more emphasis on proper soffit installation in high-wind regions. • **FL-10b.** The FBC should require soffit inspections.

4.4.8 Ground-Mounted Photovoltaic Systems

The Texas, USVI, and Puerto Rico MATs observed extensive damage to ground-mounted photovoltaic systems caused by under-designed structural support and connectors. In the USVI and Puerto Rico, the damage was severe and there were many challenges to restoration, so the full return of electrical utility service was delayed. See Section 3.2.5.1 for details about MAT observations of ground-mounted photovoltaic system performance during the 2017 hurricane season. Table 4-16 presents the MAT conclusions and recommendations related to ground-mounted photovoltaic systems.

Table 4-16: Ground-Mounted Photovoltaic Systems

Conclusions	Recommendations
PR-38, USVI-33. Ground-mounted PV systems heavily damaged by the storm hindered the full return of electrical utility service.	**PR-38, USVI 33.** Incorporate mitigation and preparedness aspects into PV system repairs.
PR-39, USVI-35. Insufficient sizing of structural members and connections contributed to damage and failures of ground-mounted PV solar arrays.	**PR-39, USVI-35.** Designers should improve the sizing of structural systems, frames, and connections for ground-mounted PV solar arrays.
PR-40, USVI-37. Open cross-section framing members on ground-mounted PV solar arrays do not have the same performance as closed cross-section members due to differences in member strength and torsional rigidity.	**PR-40, USVI-37.** Designers should consider using closed shape cross-sections for the design of structural framing members.
PR-41, USVI-39. Installation of arrays does not allow for bolt checks, and bolt checks are generally not performed after initial construction/installation of the array.	**PR-41, USVI-39.** Ground-mounted PV solar installation and O&M procedures should account for proper bolt torque specifications and checks.
PR-42, USVI-38. Vibrations from dynamic, cyclical loading caused failure of bolted connections of ground-mounted PV solar arrays.	**PR-42, USVI-38.** Designers should consider using a stainless-steel locking nut with a nylon insert for all bolted structural connections of ground-mounted PV solar arrays.
PR-43, USVI-36. Current design standards for ground-mount PV solar arrays do not provide for dynamic testing.	**PR-43, USVI-36.** Consider research into dynamic testing of ground-mounted PV solar arrays.
PR-44, USVI-34. Current design standards do not provide recommended design loads specific to ground-mounted PV solar arrays.	• **PR-44, USVI-34a.** ASCE should consider adding specific design criteria for ground-mounted PV solar arrays to ASCE 7-22 and reference them in other select codes. • **USVI-34b.** Assign Risk Category affecting design for ground-mounted PV.

4.4.9   Rooftop Systems and Solar Equipment

The Texas, USVI, and Puerto Rico MATs observed that equipment located on rooftops was vulnerable to wind hazards and sustained damage that left buildings without key services occupants depend on such as power, HVAC, elevators, and other necessities. See Section 3.2.5.2 for details about MAT observations of rooftop systems and solar equipment during the 2017 hurricane season. Table 4-17 presents the MAT conclusions and recommendations related to rooftop systems and solar equipment.

Table 4-17: Rooftop Systems and Solar Equipment

Conclusions	Recommendations
PR-31. Debris that damaged roof coverings often was from the building itself.	**PR-31.** Adequately anchor HVAC and other equipment to roofs.
USVI-27, TX-14. Inadequate anchoring of rooftop equipment caused unnecessary damage to roof systems and building contents.	• **USVI-27, TX-14a.** Adequately anchor HVAC and other equipment to roofs. • **TX-14b.** FEMA should ensure that securing roof-mounted equipment is incorporated into eligible Public Assistance Hazard Mitigation Proposals.
PR-32, USVI-29. Building systems—including backup power generators, switches, and equipment, and fire alarm systems—should be protected against wind, wind-borne debris, and flood.	**PR-32, USVI-29.** Protect building systems to requirements of ASCE 7 and ASCE 24.
PR-33, USVI-28. Failure of equipment penthouses and elevator equipment vents on roofs caused loss of operations.	• **PR-33a, USVI-28.** Design mechanical penthouses and equipment housing to resist high winds. • **PR-33b.** Retrofit mechanical penthouses and equipment housing in existing buildings.
PR-45. Current design standards do not clearly provide recommended design loads specific to solar water heaters.	**PR-45.** ASCE should consider adding specific design criteria for solar water heaters to ASCE 7-22.

4.4.10 Shelters

Both the USVI and Puerto Rico MATs observed a lack of shelters designed in accordance with FEMA P-361 or ICC 500 for protection for residents during hurricanes. Many of the buildings used as emergency shelters and refuge areas during Hurricanes Irma and Maria were not evaluated by design professionals for flood, wind, and seismic vulnerabilities, potentially leaving occupants vulnerable. See Section 3.3 for details about MAT observations of shelter performance during the 2017 hurricane season. Table 4-18 presents the MAT conclusions and recommendations related to shelters.

Table 4-18: Shelters

Conclusions	Recommendations
PR-34. The Puerto Rico Department of Housing (Departamento de Vivienda) (PRDOH) shelter program is helpful but has shortcomings.	• **PR-34a.** PRDOH should consider updating the shelter program in accordance with FEMA guidance. • **PR-35b.** FEMA should work with PRDOH to improve the evaluation form for the PRDOH shelter program.
PR-35, USVI-31. The MAT observed no shelters designed in accordance with FEMA P-361 or ICC 500 for protection for residents during hurricanes.	• **PR-35a, USVI-31a.** Require specific educational and first responder facilities to provide a storm shelter. • **PR-35b.** Federally funded grantors for safe rooms, such as HUD, should consider requiring that FEMA 361 criteria be met. • **PR-35c, USVI-31c.** Encourage residents to build in-residence storm shelters. • **PR-35d.** Encourage municipalities and residents to create a system for identifying and tracking residential safe room and storm shelter locations. • **USVI-31b.** The Virgin Islands Territorial Emergency Management Agency (VITEMA) should consider registering public storm shelters designed to ICC 500 when they are constructed.
USVI-32. Many buildings currently being used as shelters and refuge areas were not evaluated by design professionals for flood, wind, and seismic vulnerabilities.	**USVI-32.** VITEMA and DPNR should consider developing a "best available refuge area" assessment program.

4.5 FEMA Technical Publications and Guidance

Table 4-19 summarizes the MAT conclusions and recommendations for updated technical publications and guidance. Best practices, technical guidance, and the improvement of building codes and standards enhance community resiliency and facilitate rebuilding efforts.

Table 4-19: Technical Publications and Guidance

Conclusions	Recommendations
PR-15, USVI-41, TX-23, FL-14. Selected FEMA Building Science technical guidance publications should be updated to incorporate lessons learned from the MAT.	• **PR-15a.** FEMA should consider translating select publications to Spanish. • **PR-15b, TX-23a, FL-14a.** FEMA should complete Guidelines for Wind Vulnerability Assessments for Critical Facilities. • **PR-15c, USVI-41a, TX-23b, FL-14b.** Update select FEMA Building Science Publications impacting coastal construction. • **PR-15d, USVI-41b, TX-23c, FL-14c.** Update the FEMA Risk Management Series guidance publications for natural hazards.
FL-15, TX-26. Many communities have difficulty implementing the Substantial Improvement / Substantial Damage requirements, especially after major disasters.	• **FL-15a, TX-26a.** FEMA should update FEMA P-758; at the same time, FEMA 213 should be updated to be consistent with the updated FEMA P-758. • **FL-15b, TX-26b.** FEMA should consider expanding existing training materials related to Substantial Improvement / Substantial Damage.
FL-16, TX 25. Future dry floodproofing design and construction can benefit from observed failures and successes.	• **FL-16a, TX-25a.** FEMA should update dry floodproofing guidance. • **FL-16b, TX-25a.** FEMA should evaluate existing dry floodproofing guidance and post-flood investigations to develop a recommendation for inclusion in ASCE 24.
TX-24. Post-Tropical Storm Allison Public Assistance Hazard Mitigation Proposals did not require post-construction certification to a specific requirement or standard.	• **TX-24a.** FEMA should make the requirements for projects developed under the FEMA Public Assistance and the Hazard Mitigation Assistance programs consistent between the programs. • **TX-24b.** Hazard Mitigation Proposals for dry floodproofing under the Public Assistance Program should be required to reference ASCE 24.

5 References

American Society of Civil Engineers (ASCE). 2005a. *Flood Resistant Design and Construction*, ASCE/SEI 24-05. Reston, VA.

ASCE. 2005b. Minimum Design Loads for Buildings and Other Structures, ASCE 7-05. Reston, VA.

ASCE. 2010. *Minimum Design Loads for Buildings and Other Structures*, ASCE 7-10. Reston, VA.

ASCE. 2014. *Flood Resistant Design and Construction*, ASCE 24-14. Reston, VA.

ASCE. 2017. *Minimum Design Loads and Associated Criteria for Buildings and Other Structures*, ASCE 7-16. Reston, VA.

Applied Research Associates, Inc. (ARA) / Federal Emergency Management Agency (FEMA) Geospatial Working Group. 2017a. "Gusts Experienced During Hurricane Irma" (personal communication).

ARA/FEMA Geospatial Working Group. 2017b. "Gusts Experienced During Hurricane Maria" (personal communication).

Energy.gov. 2018a. "Puerto Rico - Building Energy Code with Mandatory Solar Water Heating". Accessed April 17, 2018. https://www.energy.gov/savings/puerto-rico-building-energy-code-mandatory-solar-water-heating

Energy.gov. 2018b. "Puerto Rico - Net Metering". Accessed April 17, 2018. https://www.energy.gov/savings/puerto-rico-net-metering

FEMA (Federal Emergency Management Agency). 2008. *NFIP Technical Bulletin 2, Flood Damage-Resistant Materials Requirements.* Available at: https://www.fema.gov/nfip-technical-bulletins

FEMA. 2010. *FEMA P-499, Home Builder's Guide to Coastal Construction.* https://www.fema.gov/media-library-data/20130726-1538-20490-2983/fema499web_2.pdf

FEMA. 2015a. *FEMA P-361, Safe Rooms for Tornadoes and Hurricanes: Guidance for Community and Residential Safe Rooms, Third Edition.* Available at: https://www.fema.gov/media-library/assets/documents/3140

FEMA. 2015b. *Highlights of ASCE 24 Flood Resistant Design and Construction.* Washington, DC. https://www.fema.gov/media-library/assets/documents/14983

FEMA. 2018a. *FEMA P-2020, Mitigation Assessment Team Report: Hurricanes Irma and Maria in Puerto Rico.* Available at: https://www.fema.gov/media-library/assets/documents/158123

FEMA. 2018b. *FEMA P-2021, Mitigation Assessment Team Report: Hurricanes Irma and Maria in the U.S. Virgin Islands.* https://www.fema.gov/media-library/assets/documents/170486

FEMA. 2018c. *FEMA P-2023, Mitigation Assessment Team Report: Hurricane Irma in Florida.* https://www.fema.gov/media-library/assets/documents/176315

FEMA. 2019. *FEMA P-2022, Mitigation Assessment Team Report: Hurricane Harvey in Texas.* Available at: https://www.fema.gov/media-library/assets/documents/158123

Harris County Flood Control District (HCFCD). 2018. *Unprecedented, Federal Briefing 2018.* Spring 2018. Available at: https://www.HCFCD.org/media/2493/hcfcdfederalbriefing2018.pdf

International Code Council (ICC). 2008. *ICC NSSA Standard for the Design and Construction of Storm Shelters.* ICC 500 2008. Washington, DC: ICC. https://codes.iccsafe.org/content/ICC5002008

ICC. 2018. *International Building Code.* Washington, DC: ICC. https://codes.iccsafe.org/content/IBC2018P2

ICC. 2018. *International Existing Building Code.* https://codes.iccsafe.org/public/document/IEBC2018

ICC. 2018. *International Residential Code.* https://codes.iccsafe.org/public/document/IRC2018

Martínez- Sánchez, O. 2018. *Impacts from Hurricanes Irma and Maria in the Caribbean.* Sidebar 7.1. [in State of the Climate in 2017]. Bull. Amer. Meteor. Soc., 99 (8), S202-S203, doi: 10.1175/2018BAMSStateoftheClimate.I.

National Oceanic and Atmospheric Administration (NOAA) National Hurricane Center (NHC). *2017a. Hurricane Irma Advisory Archive.* [National Hurricane Center Public Advisories, August 30-September 9]. Available at: https://www.nhc.noaa.gov/archive/2017/IRMA.shtml

NOAA NHC. 2017b. *Irma Graphics Archive: 5-Day Forecast Track, Initial Wind Field and Watch/ Warning Graphic (webpage).* Available at: https://www.nhc.noaa.gov/archive/2017/IRMA_graphics.php

NOAA NHC. 2017c. *Maria Graphics Archive: Initial Wind Field and Watch/Warning Graphic* (webpage). Available at: https://www.nhc.noaa.gov/archive/2017/MARIA_graphics.php

NOAA NHC. 2017d. *Hurricane Maria Advisory Archive.* National Hurricane Center Public Advisories, September 16-22, 2017. Available at: https://www.nhc.noaa.gov/archive/2017/MARIA.shtml

NOAA NHC. 2018a. *Costliest U.S. Tropical Cyclones Tables Updated.* Available at: http://www.nhc.noaa.gov/news/UpdatedCostliest.pdf

NOAA NHC. 2018b. *2017 Atlantic Hurricane Season.* Accessed 29 March 2019. Available at: https://www.nhc.noaa.gov/data/tcr/index.php?season=2017&basin=atl

NOAA NHC. 2018c. *National Hurricane Center Tropical Cyclone Report Hurricane Harvey (AL092017) 17 August – 1 September, 2017.* Prepared by Eric S. Blake and David A. Zelinksy. May 9, 2018. Available at: https://www.nhc.noaa.gov/data/tcr/AL092017_Harvey.pdf.

NOAA NHC. 2018d. *National Hurricane Center Tropical Cyclone Report Hurricane Irma (AL112017) 30 August – 12 September, 2017.* Prepared by John P. Cangialosi, Andrew S. Latto, and Robbie Berg. June 30, 2018. Available at: https://www.nhc.noaa.gov/data/tcr/AL112017_Irma.pdf

NOAA NHC. 2019. *National Hurricane Center Tropical Cyclone Report Hurricane Maria (AL152017) 16-30 September 2017.* Prepared by Richard J. Pasch, Andrew B. Penny, and Robbie Berg. February 14, 2019. https://www.nhc.noaa.gov/data/tcr/AL152017_Maria.pdf

NOAA National Weather Service (NWS). 2017. *Tropical Winds Newsletter – Fall 2017.* Available at: http://noaa.maps.arcgis.com/apps/MapJournal/index.html?appid=c712badd484c4a9d8dbaa3692ba7d1fe&_sm_au_=iVVqtf7Tr510QTRn.

NOAA NWS. 2018. *Detailed Meteorological Summary on Hurricane Irma* (webpage). Tallahassee, FL, Weather Forecast Office. Available at: https://www.weather.gov/tae/Irma_technical_summary.

NOAA NWS Corpus Christi. 2018. *Hurricane Harvey Aug 25-27, 2017.* Presentation by John Metz – Warning Coordination Meteorologist. Available at: https://www.weather.gov/media/crp/Hurricane_Harvey_Summary_Rockport.pdf.

OGPe. 2017. *Administrative Order 2017-07*. October 6. http://jp.gobierno.pr/Portals/0/Ordenes%20Administrativas/Orden%20Administrativa%20OGPe-2017-07.pdf?ver=2017-10-06-075843-490

PRPB (Puerto Rico Planning Board). 2010. *Administrative Order JP-OA-2010-02*. http://jp.pr.gov/Reglamentos/Reglamentos-Planificaci%C3%B3n

PRPB. 2017. *History*. JP.PR.gov http://jp.pr.gov/Conócenos/Historia

PRPB Audit and Compliance Bureau. 2017. *Application Package for Hazard Mitigation Grant Program 4336-DR-PR (Hurricane Irma) and 4339-DR-PR (Hurricane Maria)*.

PRPB. not dated. *Construction Permit*. Integrated Permitting System (Sistema Integrado de Permisos). Accessed August 17, 2018. https://www.sip.pr.gov/web/guest/ciudadano/permisos/permisos-obra/construccion

Resilient Puerto Rico Commission. 2018. *Housing Briefing Document*. Available at: https://www.resilientpuertorico.org/wp-content/uploads/2018/03/Housing-Working-Group-Document-Brief-.pdf

U.S. Virgin Islands Department of Natural Resources (USVI DPNR). 1996. *Construction Information for a Stronger Home*.

USVI DPNR. 2018. *Construction Information for a Stronger Home*, 4th Edition. Available at: http://www.vitema.vi.gov/docs/default-source/response-recovery-documents/(1)-construction-information-for-a-stronger-home-4th-edition.pdf?sfvrsn=c52995d_2

Appendix A:
2017 MAT Reports and

COMPENDIUM REPORT
2017
HURRICANE SEASON

Recovery Advisories

FEMA's Hurricanes Harvey, Irma, and Maria (2017) webpage provides links to the MAT reports and recovery advisories developed in response to the 2017 storms.

FEMA P-2020, Mitigation Assessment Team Report: Hurricanes Irma and Maria in Puerto Rico: The Puerto Rico MAT assessed the performance of residential, nonresidential, and critical facilities; evaluated the performance of photovoltaic (PV) facilities; the effects of wind speed-up due to the islands' topography on building performance; and met with residents and local officials to better understand what transpired during and after Hurricanes Irma and Maria. The Puerto Rico MAT also developed the following recovery advisories:

PR-RA 1: Rooftop Equipment Maintenance and Attachment in High-Wind Regions

PR-RA 2: Siting, Design, and Construction in Coastal Flood Zones

PR-RA 3: Safe Rooms and Storm Shelters for Life-Safety Protection from Hurricanes

PR-RA 4: Best Practices for Minimizing Flood Damage to Existing Structures

PR-RA 5: Protecting Windows and Openings in Buildings

PR-RA 6: Repair and Replacement of Wood Residential Roof Covering Systems

FEMA P-2021, Mitigation Assessment Team Report: Hurricanes Irma and Maria in the U.S. Virgin Islands: The USVI MAT evaluated damage from Hurricanes Irma and Maria, especially for buildings constructed or reconstructed after Hurricane Marilyn (1995), to identify both successful and unsuccessful mitigation techniques. This work involved: assessing the performance of residential, nonresidential, and critical facilities affected by the storms; evaluating the performance of photovoltaic (PV) facilities; investigating the effects of wind speed-up due to the islands' topography on building performance; and meeting with residents and local officials to better understand what transpired during and after Hurricanes Irma and Maria. The USVI MAT also developed the following recovery advisories:

USVI-RA 1: Rebuilding Your Flood-Damaged House

USVI-RA 2: Attachment of Rooftop Equipment in High-Wind Regions

USVI-RA 3: Installation of Residential Corrugated Metal Roof Systems

USVI-RA 4: Design Installation and Retrofit of Doors, Windows, and Shutters

USVI-RA 5: Rooftop Solar Panel Attachment: Design, Installation, and Maintenance

FEMA P-2022, Mitigation Assessment Team Report: Hurricane Harvey in Texas: The Texas MAT was deployed to Harris County to assess flood performance issues, and to Aransas, Nueces, Refugio, and San Patricio Counties to assess wind performance issues. MAT members evaluated building systems to determine the effectiveness of various design and construction practices and ascertain the effect of code adoption and enforcement on reducing flood and wind damage. The Texas MAT also developed the following two recovery advisories:

TX-RA 1: Dry Floodproofing: Planning and Design Considerations

TX-RA 2: Asphalt Shingle Roofing for High-Wind Regions

FEMA P-2023, Mitigation Assessment Team Report: Hurricane Irma in Florida: The Florida MAT assessed the performance of municipal buildings, coastal residential properties, and public facilities to make recommendations for actions that Federal, State, and local governments; the design and construction industry; and building code and standards organizations can take to mitigate damage from future natural hazard events. The Florida MAT also developed the following three recovery advisories:

FL-RA 1: Dry Floodproofing: Operational Considerations

FL-RA 2: Soffit Installation in Florida

FL-RA 3: Mitigation Triggers for Roof Repair and Replacement in the 6th Edition (2017) Florida Building Code

www.ingramcontent.com/pod-product-compliance
Lightning Source LLC
Chambersburg PA
CBHW080053280326
41934CB00014B/3301